PUBLISHED BY:
THE HERITAGE CLASSIC FOUNDATION
79 LIGHTHOUSE ROAD
HILTON HEAD ISLAND, SOUTH CAROLINA 29928

DESIGN AND ART DIRECTION BY KELLY L. GRAHAM, HILTON HEAD ISLAND, SC

PRODUCTION AND EDITING COORDINATION BY CHERNOFF/SILVER & ASSOCIATES

PRINTING BY STEIN PRINTING COMPANY, ATLANTA, GA

COPYRIGHT ©1995 BY THE HERITAGE CLASSIC FOUNDATION

PRINTED IN THE UNITED STATES OF AMERICA

1ST PRINTING, 1995

LIBRARY OF CONGRESS CATALOG CARD NUMBER 95-079739

ISBN 0-9645831-0-0

# MCI Classic
## The Heritage Of Golf

# A Tournament Retrospective

## by Vance Fowler
### Foreword by Arnold Palmer

# INTRODUCTION
# BY ARNOLD PALMER

A little more than 26 years ago, I received an invitation to sign up for a tournament named the Heritage, to be played on a course called Harbour Town. The names "Heritage" and "Harbour Town" were unfamiliar to me — as well as to most of the fellow golfers I talked to. But that was not peculiar because the tournament had never been played before and, in fact, the course itself was still unfinished. Furthermore, the play was to take place during Thanksgiving week, at the tail end of a long season.

If curiosity killed the cat, as the old saying goes, I would be dead a dozen times over, because I'm always curious about places I have never been and courses on which I have never played. Yet I had an urge to see for myself and decided I might just have to go on down there to this island called Hilton Head in what has long been referred to as the Lowcountry. There was one further incentive. My old friend and frequent adversary, Jack Nicklaus, was involved — but not so much as a competitor as one of the planners of the course itself. That was something new, and again I was nosy enough to want to find out just what was in the works with Jack.

To make a long story short, I did sign up for that first Heritage and I did get to Hilton Head Island and I did spend the better part of a week ranging far and, fortunately, not too wide over the Harbour Town Links. It was one of the most memorable experiences in my life and one of the most pleasurable as well. The location was right out of a picture book, the islanders were hospitable and charming, the accommodations were comfortable, the fans were enthusiastic and the events were unbelievably well-organized for a tournament that was in its infancy.

After the final round was over, I came away with the feeling that I wanted to come back and I hoped the tournament would be a smashing success in years to come. I had good reason to be happy with my decision, and the experiences that resulted from it. But that is all part of the story of an event that has become known as the MCI Classic - A Heritage of Golf, a course named the Harbour Town Golf Links, and a place called Hilton Head Island. If you want to know more, just read on.

This volume on the history of the MCI Classic - A Heritage of Golf tournament is, in effect, an in memoriam to the late Vance Fowler, who for a period of 25 years, from 1969 to 1993, served as the volunteer announcer on the ninth green. Except for the very first day of the very first tournament, he never missed a day — whether because of illness, weather, or any other reason — and thus became the individual who was probably the best known of all of the thousands of volunteers who have served at this splendid annual golfing event.

Vance was an ardent history buff and was always very much interested in the island and its institutions, and particularly the tournament itself and its background. He devoted many years to this field of interest and, a year or so before the Silver Anniversary of the tournament, in 1993, decided that he would research and write the history of what many still fondly refer to as "The Heritage", despite several name changes over the years. Vance was deeply immersed in this project at the moment of his untimely death in late 1993. It is perhaps significant that he, as a naval officer who was almost killed during the Japanese attack on Pearl Harbor December 7, 1941, should have died on that very day 52 years later.

It was the decision of the Heritage Classic Foundation to review the draft of the very detailed historical manuscript authored by Vance and to distill from it the essence of his writings, which have formed the text for this book. We hope that it will serve as a fitting commemoration, as well as a tribute to all of the volunteers who have helped to make "The Heritage" what it has become in the world of golf, and in the hearts of the contenders and the spectators alike.

*Vance Fowler announced for 25 consecutive years.*

# CONTENTS

# CHAPTER 1
# THE ORIGINS OF A GOLF CLASSIC

*Arnold Palmer's 1969 victory gained national recognition.*

IN MID-JULY, 1968, selected sports reporters in newspapers and golf periodicals received telegrams announcing a new tournament, the Heritage Golf Classic, which was being sponsored jointly by Delta Airlines and Sea Pines Plantation. Described as "the first major professional golf tournament to be held directly on the Atlantic seacoast," the Heritage was to be launched during the week of November 25 to December 1 that year, on Hilton Head Island at the southernmost tip of South Carolina. The telegram was signed by one William Dyer, the first executive director of the tournament.

Golfing journalists were in for some surprises. The first was that the Heritage was no Johnny-come-lately, but indeed had a blue-blood ancestry of its own, commemorating the issue of a charter to the historic South Carolina Golf Club, the first in America, founded in Charleston in 1786. The second eye-opener came when a follow-up telegram at the end of the summer announced that the Heritage would not be scheduled that year, after all, but would be held in the late fall of 1969 on a brand new course to be designed and built at Harbour Town, in Sea Pines Plantation. In the opinion of many people in the golfing world, it was an

*The 1969 Pro-Am trophy.*

ambitious dream to expect to complete an 18-hole course, of tournament quality, in just over a year, attract a top-ranking field, and draw a proper throng of spectators. Furthermore, few pros or PGA Tour officials were familiar with the work of Pete Dye, the almost unknown golf architect who had been assigned the task.

Those who planned this major event had the foresight to persuade Jack Nicklaus to act as a consultant in the design of the course, and to encourage many prominent golf professionals to sign up for the initial Heritage

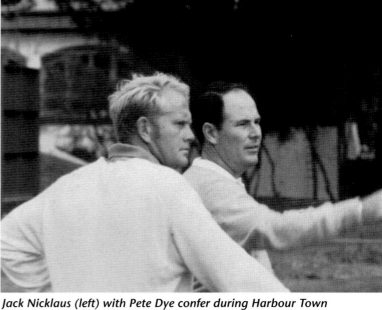

*Jack Nicklaus (left) with Pete Dye confer during Harbour Town Links design.*

field. The happy outcome was that the course really was finished in time — though barely — and that the first Heritage tournament was successfully held at a most unlikely time of the year, Thanksgiving week, 1969. The astonishment of the critics and skeptics was aptly summed up in an article that appeared in Sports Illustrated a week later. "In a dolled-up swamp off the coast of South Carolina's low country and on an island with more dripping moss and crooked magnolias than you would find in a dozen Civil War novels," wrote sports editor Dan Jenkins, "Jack Nicklaus made his debut as a golf course designer last week before the toughest possible audience — his fellow touring pros. These included his friendly rival, Arnold Palmer, who seized the occasion to show Jack and everybody else how the magnificent course ought to be played.

"It was a unique Thanksgiving holiday for professional golf. The fact that there was any sort of tournament being played anywhere in the midst of so much football frenzy around the country must have caught thousands of people by surprise. There was nothing in the TV log about it, right? Right. What was this Heritage Classic, anyhow? And where is this Hilton Head Island where Nicklaus had carved out a course among trees and marsh and where Palmer had done that thing he used to do so often? Like win."

"Well, the Heritage was a regular PGA Tour event played on a new layout called the Harbour Town Golf Links, and it was worth $100,000, as were many of those other classics that come and go. But aside from these things, it had a good many distinctions that are likely to make it a true-to-life mini-classic of the fall golf season, not the least of which is the simple fact that it will be remembered as the tournament, course and resort where America's favorite hard body, Palmer,

"All of Harbour Town's par-3s are memorable, but the most famous — and most difficult — hole is a par-4, the marvelously scenic, horribly treacherous 18th. If there's one hole that should have a graveyard, this is it .... If there's one advantage, it's that you can aim your approach shot at a red-and-white-striped lighthouse that ads charm and character to the setting."

**Hubert Mizell, quoted in "Great Golf Courses of the World," by the editors of Golf Digest.**

came back from bad times to win a tournament."

The first Heritage was not only a sporting success, but Harbour Town was described by Sports Illustrated as "just about the best new course that anyone has built in ages, a brutally narrow, abruptly twisting table of brooding pines, oaks, palmettos and magnolias with tiny greens guarded by wriggling bunkers and fierce marshes . . . Nicklaus and his partner, Pete Dye, have given us nothing short of a work of art."

As was also pointed out by several sports writers, the timing of the tournament was totally at odds with reality. In 1969, the essential part of the PGA Tour had been completed Labor Day weekend when the World Series of Golf was played at Firestone. Fall was considered no time to compete with the baseball World Series, college and pro football and the heavy television offerings they provided. There simply was no room for golf. Why would anyone even think of conducting a top-class golf tournament — at Thanksgiving, no less? One of the extraordinary facts behind the Heritage concept was that one of its most dynamic pioneers had been Charles Fraser, who is not a golfer to begin with.

*1970 winner Bob Goalby (right) with 1971 tournament director Dave Albaugh (left) and Laurie Auchterlonie - Honorary Golf Professional at St. Andrews in Scotland.*

Charles was known as an innovative developer who had faced doubters countless times while he turned what was at first a mosquito-infested, unknown wetlands into one of the finest resorts in the Americas: Hilton Head Island.

Even taking into consideration the fact that the promoters were rash enough to think they could conduct a golf tournament under such contradictory conditions, how could they possibly line up top-ranking players at Thanksgiving? Even the most dedicated competitors would be looking forward to a traditional family celebration at home. But Charles Fraser's fertile mind anticipated that many players on the Tour would be intrigued by the idea of playing on a course where their popular peer, Jack Nicklaus, had assisted Pete Dye in its unique design and construction. A further incentive was that Arnold Palmer had earlier displayed an interest in the courses the island had to offer, and needed only a bit of urging from Jack to be drawn into the fold. Recruiting others became easier when they learned that both Jack and Arnie would be playing.

The entire event was presented as a vacation for players and their families, in comfortable housing near the golf course and with all the amenities and attractions of a most magnificent natural environment. The combined appeal proved to

be effective enough so that in no time at all the file had grown to include such golf luminaries as George Archer, Julius Boros, Homero Blancas, Dow Finsterwald, Lionel Hebert, Davis Love, Jr., Bob Murphy, Lee Trevino and Tom Weiskopf, among others.

The first Heritage, despite its favorable reviews in the press, was anything but a monetary success. In fact, had an accurate financial forecast been publicized, the Heritage might have ended before the course was even laid out. As history reveals, it was to be 15 years before the financial picture would get into the black, a position it has fortunately maintained since then.

## THE FIRST TOURNAMENT

Most people remembering the first tournament think only of the dramatic moments of play as Arnold Palmer turned his hesitant playing around on the third day and went on to win. But the events behind the scenes were, if anything, even more suspenseful. Having allowed only 13 months in which to build the Harbour Town Golf Links, it was with deep concern that those involved awaited the November 4, 1969, visit of Joseph C. Dey, Jr., Commissioner of the Tournament Players Division of the PGA. Dey was to determine whether the impossible had been achieved, making the course qualified for play barely three weeks hence — a frightening prospect for the small band of Heritage pioneers.

*A young Jack Nicklaus practices early on 9th green with Harbour Town Clubhouse still under construction.*

Those close to the situation knew that, in spite of their Herculean efforts, some parts of the course might not yet meet Tour standards. A major trouble spot was a portion of the second green, where grass was an unknown commodity. It was too much to hope that the trained eye of the inspector would miss the bald spots. But the considerate Commissioner suggested that heavy quantities of rye grass seed and pine straw could do wonders for the course's appearance, even commenting, "I found it to be a great course with some truly classic holes." When approval was given for the Thanksgiving Day start on November 27, the Heritage committee members were jubilant.

For the players arriving on the island for the very first time, Hilton Head was a brand new experience. On the occasion of the Silver Anniversary of the Heritage, Ron Cerrudo, director of golf instruction at the Shipyard Plantation, recalled his first impressions in 1969. He had been on the tour for two years when he arrived at night at the Savannah Airport. "It was pitch black," he said. "It seemed as though we drove forever. The first thing I remember — and it seemed pretty strange at the time — were the lighted palmettos along the highway at the Jones course at Palmetto Dunes. Most of the tour players had no idea where Hilton Head was. Someone just pointed us in the direction of the tournament and we went." Although Cerrudo missed the cut by one stroke, he had strong impressions of Harbour Town in 1969. "The course was tough, but I liked it. I had never played a course quite like it. Even then, I felt there was something about Hilton Head. This is where you came to play golf. You could feel it everywhere."

*The Scottish Heritage has been captured in many ways.*

Like Cerrudo, many players were intrigued by the mystery of an island that was completely unknown to them. "The 1969 Heritage was a watershed for Hilton Head," wrote author Paul deVere in an article on the 25th anniversary. "While it is true that when the Heritage was first televised a few years later, the world 'discovered' Hilton Head, that first tournament helped Hilton Head Island discover itself."

What the visiting pros seem to remember most collectively from the early years of the Heritage is that Hilton Head was a friendly place and not some kind of rich man's "Fantasy Island" hideaway. The relationship worked both ways as the islanders got to know the visiting pros, many of whom brought their families along for a brief vacation. Donald O'Quinn, who was vice president of sports for Sea Pines and the tournament's first manager, recalls that lasting friendships were made because many players on the tour had to stay as guests in private homes, since public accommodations were very limited. He and his wife, Dot, not only helped with "room assignments," but hosted an oyster roast that was one of the tournament's early highlights, bringing visitors and islanders together.

*Dawn at the first tee, November 1969.*

Although normally the weather on Hilton Head is pleasant around Thanksgiving time, such was not the case in 1969. The skies were nasty and the temperature so frigid that the Pro-Am had to be reduced to nine holes when frozen greens resulted in a late start. The Pro-Am did, however, produce one incident which says a great deal about the integrity of the game of golf. Kermit Zarley started the 18th hole with a superb drive that rolled slightly into the right rough. His expert second shot saw the ball landing barely three feet from the pin. But as Kermit turned from the spot where he had hit this shot, he detected another golf ball on the edge of the rough. To his dismay, examination disclosed that the ball was a Spalding Black Dot #1, the same ball he was playing. Although he felt certain he had hit his own ball, and although all members of the foursome concurred, Kermit knew only too well the strict rules of golf. He was obligated to identify his ball without question — and this he could not do. Since both balls were Spalding Black Dots #1, and not otherwise marked in any way, he had no alternative but to disqualify himself for the 18th hole. Although Kermit's team remained in play his routine birdie was sorely missed. This episode demonstrates that the ethics of golf are higher than those of a well-known professional football coach who was reported to have said, "Winning isn't everything, it's the only thing!"

Despite the uncooperative weather, 138 players teed up on that fateful Thanksgiving morning, starting on both the 1st and 10th holes because of the shortage of daylight hours. The big question was, "Who has the best chance of winning?" There were a lot of guesses, but not too many meaningful answers when trying to judge the pitfalls and advantages of an unknown course. While many voiced the opinion that either Jack or Arnold would be popular winners, it was unlikely that either could be victorious. Almost certainly, Jack's playing efforts would be affected negatively by his continuous preoccupation with course details. As for Arnold Palmer, he was at the time regarded as one of the longest straight drivers on the tour. But he had not won a tournament in 14 months and was struggling with putting problems that were at least partially responsible for his long period of drought. By contrast, prior to his dry spell, he had averaged four victories a year for some 13 years. One national magazine was so insensitive as to suggest in an editorial that, "Arnie may be over the hill."

*Three-time winner Hale Irwin, shown here in 1974, played in the 1969 tournament and missed the cut. He has played in all but one Heritage since then.*

But Arnie's charisma was still there, his inimitable swagger, the way he customarily hitched up his trousers while evaluating a situation, and then his characteristically daring approach to play, all qualities that endeared "The General" to his "army." Local golf writer Terry Bunton characterized him as a popular hero because he was "the boy next door, a combination of Jack Armstrong and Horatio Alger. He came from a small town, of humble origins, worked hard, and made good." The gallery was always excited watching him play because he frequently threw caution to the winds and attempted bold strokes that other players would have averted.

That cold Thanksgiving day warmed up as Arnie birdied on two after missing an eagle, made a birdie putt of 12 feet on the fourth hole, and sank a five-foot birdie putt on the fifth. His only bogey of the day came on eight. That gave him a two-under 34 for the front nine. A 20-footer on ten was to be his final birdie of the day, as he finished with eight pars for a very respectable three-under 68. Tied for the lead was George Archer who equalled Arnie's score of 34-34-68.

Jim Colbert, who was one stroke behind, called the Harbour Town Golf Links "the toughest course we've played all year." Jack Nicklaus, who fired an even par 71 on the course that he had helped build, stated in semi-shock, "Eight guys under par, I can't believe it." Before the tournament was over, Jack's "belief" would be restored. Only the winner would wind up par or better.

*Past champions gathered to honor the tourney's 25th anniversary.*

Daybreak the second day saw Tom Weiskopf off to a gloomy start. But, looking for his first victory in more than a year, he played through light, almost steady rain, to record a course record of 32-33-65 by the time he finished shortly before noon. Weiskopf attributed his excellent 27-putt round to the rainy conditions. "I always putt better with moisture on the greens," he joked. "I can see the line more clearly."

Meanwhile, Arnie was progressing quite well. Playing in a cold, steady drizzle, Palmer had this to say, after firing a 71, "I always felt that I could get through my bad round, and I consider today a bad round. Maybe my next two will be as good as yesterday's." Although he had to birdie two of the last six holes to make it to even par, he was not aware of the fact that he did not need to play better to win. Meanwhile, young Richard Crawford's 69 and George Archer's 73 brought third place, one-under, ties for the pair, two shots behind the first place tie of Palmer and Weiskopf.

When reviewing Tom Weiskopf's record-setting round that day, Pete Dye proved himself a better architect than prognosticator. Pete predicted there would be many low scores in the future. Such has not been the case. Actually, it would not be until six tournaments later, in 1975, when in the second round a fired-up Jack Nicklaus would beat the record with an eight-under 63. Denis Watson in 1984 was the next to tie Jack's record, followed by Jim Hallet in 1988 and Ray Floyd in 1992.

Low scores are the exception, not the rule, at a still very demanding Harbour Town Golf Links. Bunton, who has chronicled the tournament since its beginning, once wrote "Harbour Town Golf Links is as enigmatic and contradictory as golf itself, ever subject to the whims of nature and ever changing, while remaining essentially the same." When questioned about an attitude a golfer needs to be a winner at the Heritage, he replied, "Both conservative and aggressive players have won at Harbour Town. The key has always been for the player to know when to attack and when to play with caution." As he has observed over the years, there are

*Young lions Johnny Miller (left), and Tom Kite were regulars in the early years.*

certain characteristics and styles of play that can augment a competitor's chances of victory on this particular course: Long hitters have no particular advantage and must, in fact, learn to exert control. The better wind players fare better than those who are bothered by gusts and changeable currents. The most consistent low scorers are the golfers who have an ability to spin the ball and play a variety of shots with a variety of clubs. The tournament's best players are the ones who regularly strike the ball solidly.

Weather, of course, throws many an accomplished player off kilter, while others (like Weiskopf) seem to relish some sort of meteorological challenge. Saturday's weather showed little improvement, characterized by cold, blustery winds and black, threatening rain clouds. Arnie was apparently better prepared for these conditions than his opponents, settling for a one-under-par 70, which gave him a three-shot lead over Richard Crawford and Bert Yancey.

Although three shots is by no means a safe margin in this caliber of golf, Arnie did not seem to be in jeopardy until the eighth and ninth holes where bogeys cut his lead to two over his close competitor, Richard Crawford. A two-time NCAA champion, Crawford, who was paired with Palmer, had not won in seven years on the Tour. Nevertheless, gloom reached its peak for the "Army" as the leader hooked his drive into the water left of the 10th fairway. But Arnie asserted his authority when his one-stroke penalty drop was followed by as pretty a five-iron shot as could ever be desired. A successful 15-foot putt preserved par and alleviated the tension, but only momentarily, when Crawford sank a 30-footer on the 11th hole for birdie. Unperturbed, Palmer calmly stroked in his own 25-foot putt and maintained his two-shot edge. The 17th hole proved decisive. Crawford hit into the left bunker and took a bogey. Palmer was off green to the right, but chipped up and sank a 9-foot putt. The glorious game was essentially over. Arnie's routine par on 18 gave him a one-under-par tournament total of 273. Crawford's bogey dropped him back to a 286 tie for second with Bert Yancey who, in later years, would be an assistant pro at Sea Pines Plantation.

The Citadel Bagpipe band burst forth in typical Scottish style. Joy reigned supreme. The impossible had happened. After 14 months of competitive fasting, Arnie had won on a brand new course named Harbour Town in a fledgling tournament called the Heritage. The inauguration had been a spirited success.

The victor was elated. "It was almost like my first win," said Palmer with a contagious grin. "This tournament was just about as hard to win as my first. And I wanted to win this one as much as if it were the U.S. Open or The Master's." Tossing a few kudos to the spectators, he added, "The gallery made me want to win. Every time I had a letdown, the fans would pump me back up." He could not resist the urge to needle his heir apparent, Nicklaus. "I would like to thank Jack for helping to build a golf course on which I could finally win one." It is unlikely that a victory by any other player could have brought as much favorable recognition to Hilton Head in the world of golf as did the unique achievement by Arnie.

In retrospect, islanders were astonished at the way in which the electricity generated by the first Heritage reached far beyond the local scene. Nationally-known golf writers, visiting as guests on a business holiday, recognized the significance of what they had just seen, found typewriters and got their message on the wire. The next day, every major American newspaper would carry the story. But this was not just national news. Papers in such diverse locations as Paris and Teheran reported the good news: Arnie's back. National magazines also provided extensive coverage, such as the earlier mentioned story that was published in Sports Illustrated. Two weeks later, Arnold

*Tom Weiskopf set a course record (32/33-65) during the second day of the inaugural event.*

Palmer was recognized as "Athlete of the Decade," with strong focus on his significant victory at the Heritage.

*The opening parade has become as much a tradition as the event itself.*

After the MCI Heritage Classic Silver Anniversary tournament in 1993, it was calculated that more than 125,000 spectators had enjoyed Heritage week. Yet, very few of these interested golf fans were aware of the birth pains, development and survival of this impressive tournament through the years. The first pioneer of the Heritage is recognized as Charles Fraser, who described himself as an historian, a golf businessman, but not a golfer by reputation. With help from his able associates, Fraser laid plans for the first golf course on Hilton Head Island in 1959 and 1960, the catalyst for all the outstanding golf courses since built on the island. In addition, others associated directly with him in these ventures have been responsible for at least 50 more of their own courses over the past two decades.

Oddly enough, Charles's lifetime sports interests have been on the water and not the links. As a youth, he spent weekends and holidays sailing and water skiing. His parents did present him with a set of clubs when he left home to go to college, but he spent more time on the campus newspaper than on the nearby course. Playing a few times at the University of Georgia and Yale Law School, he was generally happy to let his clubs gather dust in the closet. After earning his law degree, he accepted a position at the leading firm in Augusta, Georgia, two of whose clients were the Augusta National Golf Club and the Master's Tournament.

In reviewing plans for the first golf links at Hilton Head's new Plantation Club, Fraser could find only four coastal golf courses between the southern bound-

*The Harbour Town Links in 1970 still looked young.*

ary of North Carolina and the northern boundary of Florida. There were two courses at Myrtle Beach, South Carolina, none on the islands near Charleston and Savannah, one at Sea Island, Georgia, and an ancient, small course on nearby Jekyll Island. Although his first master plan for Sea Pines included only a single course, a number of landowners on the island thought it was superfluous — and said so.

It was through the Augusta law firm that he became acquainted with a member of Augusta National, James Self, Jr., of Greenwood, South Carolina, the head of one of the South's major textile manufacturing companies. Jim persuaded Charles that a course would help to "type" Hilton Head as a resort and, consequently, should be a fine 18-hole layout. At a lunch during the Master's Tournament, an agreement was outlined whereby Self and a group of five associates would finance the completion of the island's first course, to be finished at one time and not in the two-step stages that had originally been advocated: nine holes one year, and the remaining nine a few years later. Construction began when there were only 42 homes in Sea Pines and 80 rooms at the Hilton Head Inn.

Local golf spectators at the first Heritage in 1969, were not as knowledgeable about golf courtesy as they are today. A lady who'd brought her own metal chair, adjusted by jangling chains, persisted in adjusting it while Doug Sanders was attempting to line up his putt. Exasperated by the clanks and jingles, Saunders walked across the green to the lady, firmly adjusted the chair in place, and sat the lady down. She smiled and thanked him, completely oblivious to the fact that she'd held up play.

At this point, the historian in Fraser took over, especially when he saw an archival reference to the South Carolina Golf Club and a list of its officers in 1786. He appointed several local archivists to probe historical records on golf and discovered historical information about the club's existence on Harleston's Green in Charleston, South Carolina. They found, among other things, numerous references to "golfer stickes" and "featheries," the name for the balls of the period, references to post-game dinner meetings at Harleston's Green, and a copy of an engraved invitation to an "Annual Golf Ball" in Savannah, Georgia, dated 1811. He then commissioned a top-ranking golf writer, Charles Price, to use this historical research to author what would eventually be a slim volume on the birth of the sport in the United States during the pre-Revolutionary period in Charleston. In this endeavor, he was assisted by George C. Rogers, Jr., Ph.D., professor of history at the University of South Carolina, who was authoring a paper on golf in his home state in the late 18th century.

The conception of the book was motivated in part by the existence of sports history books authored by New Yorkers, which claimed that golf in America began in Yonkers, New York, in 1868. It aggravated Fraser and his colleagues to read

Yankee descriptions of golf clubs in the South as being nothing more than social gathering places.

Charles Price moved to Hilton Head while engaged in his research and writing, and became increasingly interested in the Sea Pines Company, which was then operating two courses. He accepted an assignment to plan a tournament proposed by the company, to be held on the Ocean Course in the fall. But this tournament was postponed from 1968 until November, 1969. Price was instrumental in this decision, insisting to Charles Fraser that the Harbour Town Course was going to be a landmark in American golfing and that it should be the site of the first tournament to be played on Hilton Head. It was at this time that another decision was made, to name the tournament "The Heritage" in recognition of the fact that the club in Charleston had been operating for some 25 years a full century before the game was ever introduced in New York.

At the suggestion of Price, the late Laurie Auchterlonie, the honorary professional at St. Andrews Golf Club in

*Galleries sharply increased when the tournament was moved from November to the last week of March.*

Scotland, was invited to become an advisor for the Heritage. He was sought after as the ideal person to recommend ways in which the new tournament could celebrate the historic relationship between golf in Scotland and in South Carolina. One of the traditions that has resulted was the "playing in" of the new Captain of Gentleman Golfers (the previous year's winner), whose first duty has been to hit a ball from the 18th fairway out into Calibogue Sound, well-announced by the shooting of an ancient cannon.

The annual ceremony begins at what was named the Liberty Oak near the Harbour Town Yacht Basin, with a parade to the 18th green, accompanied by the piercing strains of bagpipes. At the opening ceremonies each year, the new Captain is presented with a replica of a "play club," a form of driver used in the 18th century. At the end of the tournament, the winner is presented with a jacket made of Heritage plaid, which is an adaptation of the red Royal Stuart tartan.

Charles Fraser was the ideal person to promote golf on Hilton Head, even though he was not an active golfer himself. He and his family had been associated with the region since the days when his father, Major General Joseph B. Fraser, had purchased some 8,000 acres of virgin forest on the southern end of the island in the decade following World War II. In 1956, with the support of his father and older

*In 1974 then Sea Pines president Jim Light led the parade with defending champion Hale Irwin and Delta Air Lines officials.*

brother, Joe, Charles planned the initial Sea Pines Plantation and, in 1957, incorporated the Sea Pines Plantation Company. Two years later, realizing that he needed to attract more people to the island to buy homesites, he financed the construction of the 80-room Hilton Head Inn with the assistance of Johnson, Lane, Space and Company of Savannah, and Liberty Life Insurance Company of Greenville, S.C. Characteristically, he insisted that this be a first-class establishment, even though room rates and meals initially had to be subsidized by the real estate firm.

Jim Self helped to underwrite the purchase of additional acreage for the new plantation, and it was during this transaction that he and Fraser discussed steps that could be taken to improve land sales. They agreed that a golf course would greatly

*Never a golfer, Charles Fraser nonetheless knew how to promote golf.*

enhance the desirability of inland home sites, and Self volunteered to help under the condition that only a first-class golf course would be constructed. Thus, the plans for the Ocean Golf Course were finalized. Self not only underwrote substantial financing, but provided heavy construction machinery from his company in Greenwood — equipment that was in place and operating within a week after he gave his verbal commitment to participate in the venture. The back nine of the Ocean Course was completed in 1960 and the front nine, a year later. The land, which had been a swamp (called a savannah by the locals), extended all the way from the ocean through the first three holes and 16, 17 and 18. A very challenging and playable course had become the patriarch of Hilton Head golf. Within a few years, it became necessary to provide a companion course, which was known as Sea Marsh.

Asked how the Heritage originated, Fraser explained that it was not part of the initial plan. "We had considered conducting a $50,000 tournament on the Ocean Course," he said, "and these plans were well underway. Following the victory of Jack Nicklaus at the 1966 Master's, we invited him to Hilton Head for an exhibition, culminated by a reception in his honor at the William Hilton Inn. I was struck by the fact that whenever we had invited political or industrial figures to receptions, they would attract only a handful of other guests at any one time. But when Nicklaus arrived on the scene, he was almost mobbed by throngs of well-wishers."

When, at one point, Nicklaus all but pleaded with Fraser to go somewhere

more quiet and get some relief, they walked up to the balcony of his room and
engaged in a less stressful conversation. The subject quickly turned to golf course design, with Nicklaus commenting that the two on Hilton Head were adequate for the average golfer, but too similar in their layout. A third course might be the answer. Jack said he was forming a partnership with a friend, Pete Dye, who, though new to the profession, had designed three courses in Ohio that were most impressive. Jack admitted that he wanted to venture into the design end of the business and would be interested in Hilton Head as a place to start, in collaboration with Dye.

*Jack Nicklaus claimed his Heritage win in 1975.*

According to Fraser, this was how Nicklaus began his new career. Jack came back to Hilton Head soon after that, bringing Dye with him. "The three of us tramped through the woods," said Charles . "Jack and Pete investigated the land near a stand of oak trees along the edge of the marsh. They surveyed the shoreline along the present site of the 17th green and 18th fairway, near the yacht basin and the promontory on which a lighthouse was to be erected." The site would be spectacular. There would be some complications, but nothing that could not be handled. At a time when most American golf courses were known for their long fairways and broad greens, Nicklaus and Dye had in mind a short course of about 6800 yards, with small greens reminiscent of the classic old courses of England and Scotland.

"We were determined to shoot for a high level," says Fraser. "I wanted a course that would, in time, have the same reputation as Pinehurst #2, Pine Valley and some of the other celebrated courses across the Untied States." Pete's response to this aspiration was, "You can do it if you keep the various committees out of our hair. We have to attempt some designs that may be considered unorthodox and we can't waste our time arguing with committees that may not see eye to eye with what we are doing. And we surely can't be kowtowing to a developer or construction manager who wonders how his swing will adapt to the new course — which is what happens in a lot of cases."

Fraser had the perfect response. "You don't have to feel threatened by me. My personal golf swing is so lousy, there's no risk of my interfering."

The design and landforming proceeded smoothly and, just as Dye had hoped, with no interference from committee members. However, midway through the construction, Pete Dye came to Fraser in consternation. The American Society of Golf Course Architects, of which he was a member, had become concerned that golf pros were being used by inexperienced or little-known golf architects as leverage to obtain contracts to build new courses. No matter how successful touring pros might be on the links, few of them had any conception of what was needed in golf course design. So the ASGCA had just passed a resolution that none of its members could use the name of a touring professional as a "co-designer" until that person had spent two years working with them to learn the trade.

"We'll have to take Jack's name out of the picture," Pete groaned, "or else I'll be kicked out of the Society."

As it turned out, Nicklaus was permitted to remain as a participant, without risk to Dye's standing, since the partnership had existed before the ruling was made and since he was listed as a consultant and not a co-designer.

*Donald O'Quinn, (far left), Sea Pines' first Director of Golf at the 17th in 1972.*

> On the first day of the first Heritage, course architect Pete Dye noted that all the players played well to the right of the large, specimen pine he'd saved to landscape the hole, effectively taking out of play a waste-bunker that Pete had provided as a feature of the hole.
>
> Defying the PGA rule that changes cannot be made in a course after a tournament has commenced, Pete made an "executive decision." Telling no one, he went out that night and, in the dark, felled and removed the tree.
>
> The PGA officials didn't notice the change and, if any players did, they didn't make note of it to officialdom.

The selection of Dye as the architect for the Harbour Town Golf Course proved to be beneficial for everyone concerned. His brilliance as a designer has since that time been demonstrated by the fact that he is the architect of many of the top 100 golf courses constructed in the 1970s and 1980s.

"In his design scheme," says the conclusion of the book, *The Carolina Lowcountry, Birthplace of American Golf*, by Charles Price and George C. Rogers, Jr., "Pete Dye looked to the natural setting of the Sea Pines site to provide intrinsic nuances to the course, utilizing the magnificent live oaks dripping with Spanish moss, the tall pines, palmettos, yucca and wire grasses, the picturesque sea marshes, and the forbidding waters of Calibogue Sound as a base of operations." Jack Nicklaus, for his part, created a few design features, but his major contribution was what was referred to in the book as "a philosophy of the game, which had developed from his years on the tour, during which he tackled scores of championship courses."

The early Heritage tournaments were not without their problems, one of which was the abrupt arrival of thousands of visitors on an island whose facilities were limited. "We had no way of knowing," recounts Fraser, "how large numbers of people would behave and function within the plantation. Nor did we know how to train people to handle traffic. We thought we could accommodate 15,000 people the first year — more than we expected would really show up. Our budget was reasonable and our purse was only $100,000. If we could sell our quota of 5,000 tickets the first year, our marketing and advertising costs would be what we could afford to pay. But we had not yet perfected adequate accounting and management techniques, and the losses were substantial." Fortunately, the Sea Pines Company was able to absorb the deficits for the first several years.

*Waste bunkers (16th hole), treacherous pot bunkers and narrow fairways exemplify Harbour Town Golf Links.*

In hindsight, all who were in any way involved in the first tournament agreed it was fortunate that the Heritage attracted so many competent volunteers, and that the various committees were really, in effect, entrepreneurships working on their own. They kept out of each other's hair and did not interfere outside of their own perimeters of responsibility. As one committee chairman analyzed the situation, "If we had been obsessed with the idea of coordinating all our activities during the first Heritages, we would have worn everyone out with meetings long before the first ball was driven off the tee."

In the history of the Heritage Classic, the 1970s phased into the 1980s with no major changes or signs of slowing down. Attendance was high, and rising; many of the most notable players on the PGA Tour were regularly packing their bags for Harbour Town; and residents throughout the island were favorably receptive to Heritage Week, despite complaints of traffic jams and overcrowding. By the middle of the 1980s, however, critical financial problems began to surface.

The seriousness of the situation was such that even The New York Times published an article in the Business section on the money crunch at Hilton Head and at least one golf magazine forecast the end of the Heritage. It was during this period of crisis — 1986/1987 — that Charles' brother, Joe Fraser, a fine golfer in his own right, and John Curry, a non-golfer, became real champions in the fight for survival.

In 1983, the Fraser family had sold the Sea Pines Company, which they had founded 26 years earlier, to the Heizer Corporation. A Heizer subsidiary, Vacation Resorts, had become the new operator of Sea Pines, but immediately met with difficulties and faced losses of about $2 million by year's end. When the losses doubled in 1984, Heizer sold Vacation Resorts in early 1985 to another developer, Bobby Ginn. John Curry tells the story in which he played such an important role. "Ginn bought Sea Pines, as well as the old Hilton Head Company, then owned by Marathon Oil, which had been temporarily in the resort business. He formed a company called Ginn Holdings in March, 1985, whose properties also included Wexford Plantation, Indigo Run and other island properties. When the transactions were completed, almost 40 percent of Hilton Head was under Ginn control.

"Ginn's style was to sell portions of the assets to his key people, with the hope they would use their credit and that soon, a rich heir would come along and buy the package, making everyone wealthy," said Curry. "Unfortunately, that did not happen and in March, 1986, a group holding preferred stock in the South Florida Bank which had invested far more than its legal limit in Ginn Holdings, bought the company. But — as happens frequently in acquisitions — the principles had a falling out." When the new owners tried to sell parts of their assets in a manner that adversely affected the payments being made to Ginn Holdings, Ginn obtained a court order preventing further sales.

The situation would have been disastrous for the island's economy and would have placed great financial stress on the resources of the Heritage had it not been for one Avron Fogelman. He was from Tennessee, a successful apartment house developer and part owner of the Kansas City Royals baseball team. He wanted to buy Sea Pines Plantation from Hilton Head Holdings, which would have improved the financial structure of the Heritage, but found his purchase proposal mired in court proceedings that had resulted from the Ginn controversy.

*The Liberty Oak in Harbour Town at sunset during Heritage Week.*

To make matters worse, the Heritage was threatened because a major investor in Hilton Head Holdings had sponsored a Senior Tour event at Harbour Town and the prize check had bounced. This incident made the PGA administrators anxious and placed the whole future of the Heritage in jeopardy.

The court ultimately agreed to let Fogelman buy Sea Pines if it could be established that a blocked sale would endanger the Heritage. And it was at this point that John Curry intervened. "I had no connection with any of the financial players," he explained. "But I was chairman of the Hilton Head Visitor and Convention Bureau, and Federal Judge Sol Blatt asked me to testify regarding the value of the Heritage to tourism and the island's economy. My job was to convince the government that the sale was vital to the economic stability of Hilton Head so the Heritage's status could be reclaimed. I stated that Fogelman had outlined some of the improvements he would make in the Harbour Town course. It was evident that he had the resources and could make everything right."

Avron Fogelman was described at the time as "a knight in shining armor," an appellation he deserved because he had surrounded himself with reliable business associates and had acquired key properties in the area where the Heritage was played. These included the Harbour, the Lighthouse and the Plantation Club (though not the Ocean or Sea Marsh courses). His fine reputation was not enough, however, to offset the problems that could jeopardize the sale, many of which did not even come to light, and which Fogelman did not know about, until the case was heard in court. By the end of the preliminary hearings, Judge Blatt announced bluntly, "Not only will I not approve this sale, but I don't believe the group managing the properties should be left in charge because it is doing a poor job. I am going to appoint a receiver, someone who can manage these properties, until we can get everything straightened out — whether it takes a few days or many weeks!"

*Misty spring mornings can play tricks on players who draw an early morning tee time.*

John Curry was asked if he would consent to become the receiver of Sea Pines Plantation assets. He was a likely choice, since he had served as the executive vice president of Sea Pines and knew all the participants in the case. The judge was convinced he could hold the organization together and work with the reliable and dedicated employees who had stuck it out with the company during this period of turmoil. Curry did agree to accept the receivership, but only on condition that his attorney would be John West.

"As a former governor, a former ambassador, a close friend of the judge, and an island resident," explained Curry, "John had the same objective that I had. We wanted to be able to introduce knowledgeable people into the proceedings, to testify on behalf of everything we represented." Curry had to make a substantial sacrifice to do what he thought was right. In addition to devoting many weeks to the assignment, he all but had to stay away from his own office and professional business for almost two years.

"Only players of championship quality will win at Harbour Town," was architect Pete Dye's prediction after a survey of the almost-completed course.

His forecast has proved out. In its first twenty-five years, only four players who had not previously won a major tournament have ever won at Harbour Town.

The case became very complex, involving bankruptcy proceedings on the receiverships Curry was responsible for: the Hilton Head Company and the Sea Pines Company. The problems were eventually resolved, thanks to the strategy that John West conceived and executed, and the participation of many others who were involved in the legal and financial struggles of the day. One last obstacle had to be cleared, however. Deane Beman, Commissioner of the PGA tour, was convinced that he and his associates should buy the Harbour Town course for the PGA Tour, a move that Curry was equally convinced should be avoided. "You could not take the 'Crown Jewel' and sell it for any price," he asserted, "and expect to uphold the value of the other properties associated with it. We knew right from the start that the Harbour Town course had to be held with all the other assets and that Sea Pines had to be sold as a complete package, the good with the bad."

*Spectators never realized how close the tournament came to its demise.*

In order to convince the Commisioner that the PGA Tour should not withdraw authorization for the Heritage because of serious financial uncertainties, John Curry, Governor John West, Joe Fraser and Mike Stevens, the Tournament Director, went to Florida to meet with him. They promised to raise a million dollars worth of credit, enough to make needed improvements on the course and to pay the purse for the tournament, which was only four months away. Forming a consortium, they met with bankers, prominent business executives, and others who could assist in his goal. The idea was to form a non-profit corporation to make certain that money committed to the Heritage would never be subject to bankruptcy proceedings. In the end, ten corporations each pledged $100,000 to secure the million-dollar line of credit.

So smoothly did this plan of action function that few people who participated in the 1987 Heritage ever suspected that any financial problem had existed.

| Harbour Town Golf Links Scorecard | | | | | | | | | | | |
|---|---|---|---|---|---|---|---|---|---|---|---|
| Hole Number | 1 | 2 | 3 | 4 | 5 | 6 | 7 | 8 | 9 | Out | |
| Par | 4 | 5 | 4 | 3 | 5 | 4 | 3 | 4 | 4 | 36 | |

| Hole Number | 10 | 11 | 12 | 13 | 14 | 15 | 16 | 17 | 18 | In | Total |
|---|---|---|---|---|---|---|---|---|---|---|---|
| Par | 4 | 4 | 4 | 4 | 3 | 5 | 4 | 3 | 4 | 35 | 71 |

*Azaleas became part of the tourney's spring procession when it was held in March.*

*Vance Fowler at his post on the 9th green in 1971.*

# CHAPTER 3
# THE HERITAGE CLASSIC FOUNDATION

T he picture of Arnold Palmer stepping up to receive his award in 1969 was completely different from the televised image of the winner that appeared on TV screens two decades later. One of the major points of dissimilarity was the presence of a tartan sea of onlookers around knickers-clad Payne Stewart as he accepted the Heritage trophy for 1989. Apart from the amount of the prize — $20,000 vs. $144,000, this was the same tournament now accepted as part of the Hilton Head Island tradition.

"Who are these plaid-jacketed figures commanding the enviable 18th green vantage point?" inquired an editorial in Hilton Head Monthly. Answering its own question, the journal went on to identify them as "civic and business leaders, many of whom stepped forward to help save the professional golf tournament when, in 1986, it became caught up in the bankruptcy maelstrom of now-defunct Hilton Head Holdings Corp."

Equally meaningful to our story, they were also recognized as the nucleus of the Heritage Classic Foundation, the non-profit group formed to take over as tournament sponsor from the old Sea Pines Plantation Company, which had followed its parent corporation into bankruptcy court. The Foundation, aptly defined as "the driving force behind the MCI Heritage Classic," was

*In 1993, then MCI President and Chief Executive Officer, Bert C. Roberts, Jr. (left) helped David Edwards celebrate his victory with South Carolina Governor Carroll Campbell and Tournament Chairman Deke DeLoach.*

formed in 1987, following the sale of the Sea Pines Company and the bankruptcy of Hilton Head Holdings. Since the Harbour Town Golf Links was an asset of the bankrupt corporation, there was great concern about the devastating effect the situation might have on the local economy. Of immediate concern was the fact that the contract to produce the Heritage Classic in April, 1987, was in imminent danger. For a time, it looked as though the tournament might have to be cancelled or, at the very least, moved from Hilton Head itself — temporarily and perhaps forever.

Disaster was in the minds of all who loved the Heritage and had played greater or lesser roles in keeping its image bright and its operations exciting. Worst fears might have been realized had it not been for the earlier-mentioned intervention of the Hilton Head group composed of Joe Fraser, John Curry, John West, and Mike Stevens, and the foresight of the PGA Tour commissioner, in seeing that a solution was possible during the discussions in his office in Ponte Vedra, Florida.

The Heritage Classic Foundation was not a unique, untried venture. In its founding, it had followed the lead of other PGA tournaments, seeking non-profit sponsors and engaging in charitable giving and other philanthropic functions. Yet there were cons as well as pros in this institution. On the positive side, the Harbour Town Golf Links was the "golden jewel," as it had been described, which the successor holding corporation would own. On the negative side, there was no assurance that this as-yet-unknown successor would be financially strong enough to maintain the golf course in the high-caliber style that was necessary for tournament play. The Heritage managers were of one mind in acknowledging that much work had to be done on the course to correct unsatisfactory conditions that had crept in as a result of neglected, or minimal, maintenance. Furthermore, Deane Beman had expressed his not unreasonable misgivings about having to deal with such a shaky financial organization. Yet, at the same time, he acknowledged his willingness to lend support to any prudent non-profit organization that could take advantage of benefits from the PGA Tour. As a result, the Heritage Classic Foundation was essentially born through the decisions and proposals made at that historic meeting in Florida.

> ■ "I get a big satisfaction out of winning on a course I had a hand in planning and designing, especially since this is the type of course on which I'm not known to play well."
>
> *Jack Nicklaus, after his first (and only) Heritage win, in 1975, with a then-course record of 271.*

Already mentioned is the fact that, after its birth and early years, the Heritage tournament lost money and had to be carried by the Sea Pines Company as a business expense. One of the revenue-producing components of a golf event is the concessions — hot dogs, soft drinks, beer, wine, shirts, hats, etc. While the Heritage itself was losing money, ironically, the commercial firms handling its concessions were making a profit.

*MCI Telecommunications Corporation came to the tourney's rescue in 1987.*

In the mid-1970's, organizers of the Heritage recognized the need to provide a means with which to involve charities from the local community with the tournament. Other tournaments across the country were announcing large donations to their local charities and the Heritage needed to get with the program. Unique to this day on the PGA TOUR, local charities now manage and operate the food concessions at the Heritage. When a spectator buys a sandwich, ice cream or beverage from one of the stands near the clubhouse or around the fairways, they're doing more than quench a thirst or appetite, they're contributing to local area charities. Organizations such as the Rotary Club, the Lion's Club, the Island Recreation Center, the Gators/Sertoma, Hilton Head Prep School, the Island School, and the Montessori School recruit members and parents to work in their stands for the good of the cause. Over $100,000 in profit is generated annually by these hard-working, community minded individuals for their charity organization.

The pride the volunteers take in their concession's performance results in some darn good food, often regarded as being some of the best food on the Tour. It's not uncommon for the professionals to forego the food served in the lavish hospitality areas around the course for one of the ol' southern style bar-b-que sandwiches at the Island School Council booth, or a juicy hamburger from that of the Lion's Club. And, if you're around the 8th green, your nose will lead you to the Rotary Club's antique wagon serving old fashioned style popcorn, fresh and piping hot. Many PGA TOUR professionals are seen walking up the 9th fairway with a bag of that popcorn in their hands.

*Volunteer-run concessions have become an integral part of the tournament, providing significant revenue to local clubs and charities.*

Since its inception in 1987, the Foundation has raised and donated more than $3 million, while at the same time maintaining the tournament's purse through its top sponsor, the MCI Telecommunications Corporation.

Although changes are made from year to year, some 11 island organizations represent the regular recipients of funds from this endeavor: The Boy Scouts, Genesis House, Hilton Head High School, Hilton Head Prep School, Hilton Head Hospital Auxiliary, Hilton Head Rotary Club, Van Landingham Rotary, Hilton Head Lions Club, Sertoma, the Island School Council and the Sea Pines Montessori School. Throughout the state of South Carolina, more than 30 other institutions are recipients of grants from the Heritage Classic Foundation.

Traditionally, the Hilton Head Hospital received the top grant, as much as $125,000, largely for the purchase of new equipment, while sizeable donations have been made to the Medical University of South Carolina, in Charleston, for such purposes as pediatric cancer treatment at MUSC's Children's Hospital. Recently, the Foundation helped the Hilton Head Cultural Council with a grant for construction of its new Cultural Arts Center, and to the Museum of Hilton Head for its new facility.

"It always gives us a great deal of pleasure," said Joseph B. Fraser, Jr., Chairman of the Foundation, "to be able to help so many worthwhile and needy causes. The awarding of grants always marks one of the happiest days of the year for the Foundation." As he noted, it is always difficult to have to turn down requests for assistance, or limit the amounts granted, but the Foundation receives

about 100 requests each year — more than twice the number that can be granted. Organizations apply for the money in the fall. A Foundation subcommittee then reviews the applications and makes recommendations to the board of trustees, which makes the final decision on who receives money, and how much. Checks are distributed at a banquet held at the end of each year.

The tournament not only benefits charitable and educational institutions, but also augments the growth and stability of Hilton Head Island business and commerce. In 1989, reports Fraser, the Foundation commissioned a university research project to determine what bearing the Heritage tournament had on the local economy. "This study indicated that the impact of the tournament on Hilton Head and the region was $20 million," said Fraser. "There could be a lot of businesses that just would not make it were it not for the Heritage."

*Galleries have grown dramatically, with more than 30,000 for the final Sunday by the early 1990s.*

The Foundation's income derives from a variety of sources, including annual ticket sales, the Pro-Am Tournament, television revenue, and significant contributions from all sponsors, but especially from MCI. Another significant source is from the efforts of the Heritage charity team, which contributes an average of about $130,000 each year to the Foundation. The largest contribution was in 1991 when the Heritage team finished first in the PGA Tour Charity Team Competition over a seven year period starting in 1986. At the conclusion of each competitive year, Tour Directors of 42 tournaments meet to select teams for the following year. Judging from the results, *MCI Classic* Tournament Director Mike Stevens has done a superlative job in choosing the team members. In the past, teams have been selected in the reverse order of the standings for the past year. This formula calls for the last place current finisher to get first choice and so on. A team finishing high one year is placed in an undesirable, less competitive position for the following year. The fact that Heritage teams have finished near the top over a period of years further attests to Mike's drafting skills.

For the 1993 season, teams were selected under a different procedure. Teams finishing one through ten in 1992 were placed at the bottom of the draw, with names of all other tournaments placed in a hat for an impartial draw. There was considerable excitement from the Hilton Head contingent after all names had been drawn from the hat except that of the Heritage Classic. It was obvious that the remaining name was indeed the Heritage. This enabled Mike Stevens to select any player on the Tour as his first choice for the Heritage team. The name of Fred Couples came first to mind since he had won $1,344,188 in 1992, placing him at the top of the money list. There, right behind him, however, was Davis Love, III, second on the money list with $1,191,630. Mike decided to select Davis Love III, then the only three-time winner of the MCI Heritage Classic and a strong local favorite, as leader of the team. He played in the Junior Heritage at Harbour Town and his father, Davis Love, II, was a participant in the first Heritage in 1969. Other members of the 1993 team included Donnie Hammond, Mark McCumber, and Jimmy Johnston, a former Georgia Tech golfer.

*Golf legend Sam Snead made an appearance in 1978 at age 62.*

Another example of the ways in which the Foundation receives both financial and organizational support is a recently developed plan for area businesses that is designed to enhance their participation. The program, coordinated with the Hilton Head Island Chamber of Commerce, called Business Partners, comprises three grades of participation: $1,000, limited to 30 businesses; $500, limited to 50 businesses; and $250, limited to 100 businesses. The packages provide a selection of patrons' badges, parking passes, advertising, and entrance passes. These partnerships generally sell out well ahead of the tournament's opening day.

People are often confused about the relationship between the organizations that manage the Heritage and all of the events, programs, and operations related to it. In the preceding chapters we have tried to show how these relationships evolved historically. Today, the overall management encompasses a unique and very workable arrangement. In a nutshell, it works this way: The local property owners own the corporation, Sea Pines Associates. SPA owns the Harbour Town Golf Links, and is responsible for its administration and maintenance. The Heritage Classic Foundation owns the contract with the PGA Tour for the management of the annual Heritage tournament, including all profits or losses resulting from its operations. In effect, the Foundation leases the course from Sea Pines Associates, paying SPA a reasonable sum for the golfers' fees

"I have a great love for this course. It's like meeting an old friend. I firmly believe that Harbour Town is one of the best courses I have ever played, not only in the United States, but outside the country as well."

*Hale Irwin, after winning his second Heritage in 1973.*

and club revenues that are obviously lost, both during the tournament and for the time prior to Heritage week required to maintain the course unused and get the fairways and greens in top condition. In addition, the Foundation contributes significantly to major maintenance additions and PGA update requirements. Hard work on the part of all parties concerned has resulted in an amicable, professional, and fortunately profitable relationship. With very few exceptions, managers of the Foundation and Sea Pines Associates have expressed complete satisfaction with the

*Hundreds of local residents serve as tournament volunteers.*

ongoing arrangement.

Most importantly, these business and professional leaders are justifiably proud of the fact that the Heritage has become synonymous with programs that improve, strengthen and educate the community. In September, 1993, with the input and strong financial support of MCI, the Heritage Classic Foundation announced that it would increase the number of college freshman scholarship recipients to 10 for 1994, and that seven of the previous year's recipients could reapply for continued financial support in their sophomore years, provided they could meet certain conditions. According to Mike Malanick, a former Hilton Head mayor and chairman of the MCI Heritage Classic Scholarship Committee, "The Foundation is committed to providing scholarships for deserving Beaufort County high school students. Giving back to the region communal opportunity in the form of educational assistance is a priority for the foundation. Based on the initial success of the program, we believe that increasing the number of $1,500 grants from seven to ten demonstrates our continued support." The scholarship program was established in December, 1992, with a $100,000 endowment funded jointly by MCI, the international telecommunications company that is the title sponsor of the MCI Heritage golf tournament, and the Heritage Classic Foundation.

There is no doubt that the creation of the Foundation was not only an economic necessity, but an inspiration in the continuing history of the Heritage.

*Hilton Head's first mayor, Ben Racusin, served as a marshal for many years.*

And then there was the Heritage Volunteer who, after being told that the workers hats were "one size fits all," tried on 21 different hats before finding one that suited her.

*Always a crowd pleaser, Arnold Palmer.*

# CHAPTER 4
# A HERITAGE OF CHAMPIONS

Among the significant developments in the Seventies was the appointment of Deane R. Beman as Commissioner of the PGA Tour, to replace Joseph C. Dye, Jr. At the age of 29, he had resigned from a prosperous brokerage insurance firm in Bethesda, Maryland, to join the PGA Tour as a full-time player. During his six-year professional career, he had won four Tournaments before hanging up his spikes to accept the position as Commissioner. Deane took over during the most explosive period in the Tour's history — a period of dramatic growth that was not anticipated at the time he participated in his first of three Heritage Classics in 1971.

Vance Fowler remembers with great amusement one dramatic moment when Beman hit a beautiful shot toward the ninth green, but just a bit too long. In those days, the observer mounds behind the ninth had not yet been constructed and the gallery ropes were close to the green. An attractive lady was the victim of the overhit when it landed directly on her chest. Deane, greatly upset, rushed to her side and was relieved to find that she was slightly bruised but otherwise unhurt. After profuse apologies, he recovered his equilibrium and went on to the tenth tee.

*Fuzzy Zoeller (left) and Hubert Green have won 4 tournaments between them.*

Local resident Wyndell Dykes, serving as a marshal at the scene, capped the incident when he announced in a loud voice, "It would be appropriate to give the lady a Purple Heart."

Her quick and witty reply was, "No thanks, I already have one!"

In the 1970's, Lee Trevino was usually good for a few belly chuckles, as well as a lot of good golf. Well-remembered was the year 1975 when Vance appeared on the ninth green at the start of the Tournament in plaid knickers. Trevino spotted him as he approached the green to get ready to play. Momentarily struck speechless, he quickly recovered and said to Vance, "My lord, what in the world are you doing wearing those things? I thought we fought the British during the Revolution so we wouldn't have to wear such get-ups!" Then he let out a hearty chuckle and wrapped his arms around Vance to assure him he was just kidding.

The origin of the knickers is a story worth telling. It was in 1974 when Vance got the idea that it would be appropriate to duplicate the dress of the wealthy cotton planters at Harleston Green, in Charleston, South Carolina, where the first golf in America was played in 1786. Unable to locate a tailor in the Low

Country who could replicate the garment accurately, he obtained a sketch showing a knickered planter at Harleston and mailed it to a New York tailor. From the tour director, he obtained sufficient Heritage plaid fabric and shipped it to the tailor, explaining that he wanted to duplicate the baggy plus fours worn by Gene Sarazen in the 1920s. The tailor had not the faintest idea what Vance was talking about until he located a photo of Gene at his stylish best and mailed it to his shop. So, for some 19 years, until they were retired after the Heritage Silver Anniversary in 1993, the same pair of knickers became a kind of trademark for the tournament.

How did Payne Stewart get into the knickers act? On the ninth green during his first Heritage appearance, he gave Vance a warm greeting at the start of the Tournament and asked, "Where did you get those knickers?" The rest is sartorial history.

No account of the Heritage Classic in the Seventies is complete without paying homage to Jack Nicklaus, always a crowd-pleaser and a real favorite with fans and participants alike. After tying for third in 1971, Jack took a leave for three years and then returned in 1975 to prove that he was the same old master. After a record-setting 271 to finish first at Harbour Town, he moved up the road to

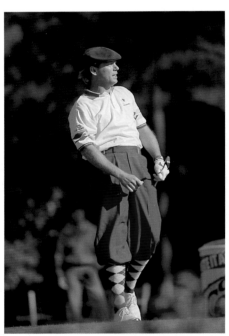

*Payne Stewart won in 1989, 1990, and 1992.*

Augusta, Georgia, where he recorded his fifth Master's win, the first four having been achieved in 1963, 1965, 1966, and 1972.

Another pleasant memory was that of Gary Player, always a gallery favorite who, despite problems arranging travel time from his home in South Africa, still found time to play in ten of our Classics. Vance particularly recalled one year when Gary went completely out of his way to walk around the greens, and bestow his appreciation for the efforts provided at the ninth green to communicate information to the gallery and whip up enthusiasm for the play and the field. Gary said that not only he, but all of the players, appreciated what the volunteers were doing for the game. It really warmed our hearts to know what a big man he was.

## THE 1970s

At the beginning of the 1970s, the Heritage producers could relax a little, with the assurance that the Heritage had been established and might survive for a few years at least. Bob Goalby won by four strokes over Lanny Wadkins, who was playing as an amateur in 1970, and at age 41 became the oldest winner in the tournament to date. Things heated up in 1971, after a rather humdrum start. There was little reason for excitement when the name of Hale Irwin was received on the entry list. He had entered the Heritage in 1969, but failed to make the cut. His 295 total in 1970 had only produced a tie for 40th position. So it was a surprise when he bested the field and came in one stroke ahead of Bob Lunn, one of the most promising young players on the Tour.

Hale proved his mettle two years later when he came back to Harbour Town in 1973. That year, for the first and only time, the Heritage was played in September, a transition agreed upon with the PGA in order that a spring date could be obtained. Irwin played magnificently — so well in his first three rounds that he entered the final round seven strokes ahead of his nearest competitor. Finishing with a one over par 72, he won with a five-stroke margin over second place finishers Jerry Heard and Grier Jones. Who could have believed he would win again 21 years later.

The year 1975 stands out because of Jack Nicklaus who, after a three year absence, was hoping to win on the course he had helped to build. A remarkable five under par 66 on the first day followed by a course record 63 on Friday clearly established Nicklaus as the man to beat. The third round was a different story. Starting with a 6-shot lead over Tom Weiskopf, he managed to accumulate 74 strokes, eleven higher than the previous day, and dropped into a tie with Weiskopf who had a 68. But in typical Nicklaus style, he returned to his usual form on Sunday, turning in a brilliant 68, three strokes ahead of Tom.

Tournament followers were in for a surprise in 1977, beginning with the arrival of Graham Marsh, a 33-year-old Australian. He was not considered to have much chance to win at Harbour Town. In the mid-1970s, foreign stars were not highly regarded by American players, and with good reason. America had been victorious in 16 of the 17 Ryder Cup Matches played between 1935 and 1975. Pros from abroad rarely appeared on the American scene and when they did, they were seldom successful. Over a period of 30 years, from 1947 to 1977, U.S. players prevailed in the three major American Tournaments, winning all but two. Marsh hoped to change all this, although he had not qualified for a PGA Tour card until four months earlier and was playing his "rookie" year. To the astonishment of many spectators, Marsh broke the jinx when his final 69 round brought a one-stroke victory over Tom Watson, despite the latter's birdie on the 18th.

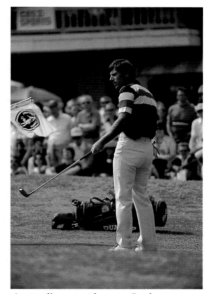

*Australian gentleman Graham Marsh outdueled Tom Watson by a stroke in 1977.*

1978 is remembered as the year of heavy fog, followed by wind gusts and rain. Hubert Green arrived at Harbour Town with the determination to repeat his victory there two years earlier. Unfortunately, his first three rounds were unspectacular, leaving him with three rounds of 70, just three under par as the final round started. That Sunday, he found himself not only five strokes behind the leader, but with five players between him and the top. Victory prospects looked dismal. While five strokes is not an insurmountable lead to overcome when only one or two players are involved, it is next to impossible to pass five in succession. However, that is just what this gutsy Alabamian did, firing a final round 67 while his challengers suc-

cumbed to the tough playing conditions of the day. He finished with a 277, two shots better than Hale Irwin.

It was significant that the Heritage's decade of the Seventies ended with a five-stroke victory for Tom Watson with a course record 270, 14 under par. More than any other player on the PGA Tour, Watson was to dominate the golf world at the end of the 1970s and the beginning of the 1980s. At the end of the tournament he said of Harbour Town Links, "I just love to play good golf on a course like this. I could play here every day, and that's the way I judge a golf course to be great."

## THE EXCITEMENT OF THE 1980s

In the history of the Heritage after more than a decade, the Seventies phased into the Eighties with no major changes or evidences of slowing down. Attendance was up, many of the best golfers on the PGA Tour were packing their bags for Harbour Town, and the whole island was increasingly receptive to Heritage Week.

*Popular Fuzzy Zoeller claimed victories in 1983 and 1986.*

Despite these rosy outlooks, 1980 was not the most memorable year for the Heritage. Strong winds blew at an increasing rate on the first day, with gusts reaching up to 30 miles an hour. If one were to have singled out one of the least likely prospects for victory, he might have picked Doug Tewell. Just the year before, this 30-year-old winless pro had decided to pack up his golf bags and look for another job. But a friend had talked him into continuing for a few more months before accepting his fate.

Jerry Pate came in with a sparkling five under par 66, despite the weather, to take the first round lead. "A helluva score, under the conditions, maybe the best of the year," remarked John Mahaffey who shared second at 68.

Conditions were even worse on Friday, and the entire day was rained out. Not wanting the Tournament to run over into Monday, PGA TOUR officials determined that after the single round on Saturday, the cut score would be reduced from the usual 70 to 50, to enable the playing of 36 holes on Sunday. But the plan was sabotaged by heavy rains Sunday morning, so only a single round could be scheduled in the afternoon. The final round was played on Monday, again in the face of the kind of weather that exhausted the players and caused error after error. Throughout it all, one player — Doug Tewell — seemed able to plug away relentlessly with some superb shots and a minimal number of lapses. On the final day, he surprised everyone by tying Pate at 280. The sudden death playoff on the par-five 15th ended rapidly as Pate hit his second shot into the water short of the green, for a bogey six. Tewell remained steady, grinding out a par five, which enabled him to achieve his first Tour victory — and enough confidence in his game to stick with it.

After Tewell proved what an underdog could do, spectators were treated to another exhibition of unheralded perseverance the following year in the person of Bill Rogers. Among the 120 players who entered the 1981 Heritage, one would have had to look long and hard to find a more unlikely winner. He had not made the cut in five of the six tournaments he entered that year and had ended up in a tie for 51st on his sole entry. His first-round par 71 attracted little attention, but he started gaining momentum on Friday with a 69, and shot 68 on Saturday, which turned out to be low round of the day and gave him a three-stroke lead.

He was in for a rude awakening though on Sunday, when Hale Irwin hit his six-iron approach shot from 166 yards for an eagle, reducing Bill's lead to one. Furthermore, Gil Morgan, Craig Stadler, and Bruce Devlin were all hot on his heels for the rest of the day. Rogers hung on, to post a 278, just one ahead of his four aggressors.

*Bill Rogers' 278 in 1981 edged four players tied for 2nd at 279 - including three time winner Hale Irwin.*

Tom Watson entered the 1982 Tournament with hopes of repeating his 1979 victory, though he was in a slump and the likelihood appeared remote. But one can never underestimate the powers of a golfer with the skill of Watson. "I made a little change in my stance and hip position," he explained. "I closed them up a bit and it gave me more freedom on my back swing." When asked the result, Watson replied, "birdie, birdie, birdie."

Playing in the group were the usual number of high-caliber contenders, like Gary Player, Fred Couples, Craig Stadler, and Tom Kite. It came as a surprise, therefore, that his chief adversary was a likeable fellow named Frank Connor — a man who had never won a Tour event and whose greatest claim to fame was that he had played in the National Open in both golf and tennis.

Weather is often a factor in determining the winner at Harbour Town and this year was to be no exception. The calm mildness of Thursday turned to a nasty blast on Sunday, when only four players were able to beat par. That weather was the worst seen in Heritage history, with the thermometer never rising above the 40's. Winds gusting to 40 miles per hour added to the discomfort of players and spectators alike. But Tom Watson, who has a reputation for playing aggressively under unfavorable conditions, was not at all perturbed by the challenge. The public relations people, who liked to extol the virtues of Hilton Head's almost perfect weather, were appalled to see the way Watson was dressed for the occasion — including a wool cap and jacket — knowing that pictures of him would be seen far and wide on TV.

*Tom Watson survived inclement weather and a sudden death playoff over Frank Connor in 1982.*

Starting the final round two shots behind Connor, Watson closed the gap to tie him at the end with a four-under-par 280. After parring the 16th and 17th holes of sudden death, they had to play into a strong wind on the 18th. Both had good drives, but Connor's approach failed to make the green and Watson, with a birdie putt, ended up the victor.

The 1983 Heritage was a landmark in that it was the first year that PGA schedules were reversed and the Heritage was played one week after the Master's tournament instead of two weeks before it. There had been concern that playing the week after The Master's would reduce the quality of the Harbour Town field. But this proved to be unfounded and it was soon evident that the good players actually enjoyed the short distance of travel between Augusta, Georgia, and Hilton Head, especially since most of them were provided with white Cadillacs for their use at The Master's, as well as to drive down to the island. Furthermore, in spite of the intensity of competition at Harbour Town, many players said that the ambience was more enjoyable and relaxing than Augusta. Consequently, the caliber of player participation continued high and even got better.

In this kind of atmosphere, Fuzzy Zoeller was right at home. One of the most colorful and likeable players on the Tour, he celebrated his tenth year of competition to win the 15th Heritage Classic in a most popular victory. His low round of 65 on Saturday placed him in an excellent position for Sunday's final. Following his well-managed 65 on Saturday, Fuzzy said, "that's the most fun I have ever had on the golf course." Zoeller and Jim Nelford were paired together on the final round and were matching stroke for stroke until Nelford ran into trouble on the 15th and 16th holes. From there on, Zoeller continued to a two-shot victory, even enjoying the luxury of a three-putt bogey on the final hole. Of Harbour Town, Fuzzy had this to say: "This course makes you think. You fall asleep and this course will eat you alive. Today, I was not trying to force the issue, and I tried to be patient."

Nick Faldo, of Hertfordshire, England, had every reason to expect respect from the press of his native land, having led the European Tour with five victories. But that was not good enough for sports writers who began to brand him "El Foldo" when he failed to achieve victories that they felt were in the bag. It was no wonder, then, that he entered the Heritage in 1984 with some misgivings, a situation that was greatly alleviated when he opened the '84 tournament in spectacular fashion with a five-under-par 66. But he had to contend with Gil Morgan who was even better with a 64. Faldo managed to get down to business and gain the lead on the second and third rounds, entering the final day with a four-shot lead over Tom Kite. His final-round 69 was good enough to fend off the fast-closing Kite's, to finish at 270 and tie the record.  With that victory, the name"El Foldo" became obsolete.

In the world of golf, achievements often seem to run in pairs.  Such was the case in 1985 when Bernhard Langer arrived at Harbour Town in 1985, fresh from a win at Augusta the week before.  Was it possible that the Heritage plaid would be donned again by a player from the other side of the Atlantic?  Possible it was, when Germany's premier golfer used his putter with exceeding skill to stay ahead of the likes of Curtis Strange, Seve Ballesteros, and Ray Floyd.  At the end of 72 holes, he was caught by Bobby Wadkins, and they headed for the 16th and sudden death.  But the playoff did not take long.  Wadkins caught the bunker on his second shot and Langer two-putted for a win, with Wadkins taking a bogey five.

The English media had put Nick Faldo under a lot of pressure, dubbing him as "Foldo" for his many late-round failures to win in the U.S. Commenting on this after his 1984 victory at Harbour Town, Nick said, "Yes, I thought about it grimly, but now, I have had the last laugh."

By 1986, it was time for an American show again, and Fuzzy Zoeller obliged with a victory over three runners-up, Chip Beck, Roger Maltbie, and Greg Norman, winning by one stroke with a 15-foot birdie.  As one newspaper account reported, "It was a peachy day for Fuzzy," not to mention his avid followers, known as "Fuzzy's Fanatics."

One of the most thrilling achievements was the one that took place in 1987.  The lists of pre-Heritage favorites did not include the name of Davis Love, III, and with sound reason.  For one thing, Love was just beginning his "sophomore" year on the Tour and was only twenty-three years old, and no player this young had ever won the Heritage.  Furthermore, Harbour Town normally does not cater to the long hitter, especially those golfers who are prone to occasional wildness.  Love's long hitting was considered one of the principal assets of his game.

However, Davis Love did have some positive things going for him.  As a teenager, he had played the Harbour Town course many times, including competition in the Junior Heritage.  In addition, he had received continuing expert instruction at home from his father, Davis Love, Jr., considered one of the top golf-

*Nick Faldo's win in 1984 was his first big win on the U.S. Tour.*

ing teachers in the nation. His father had played in the first Heritage in 1969 and was familiar with the pitfalls of the Harbour Town course — knowledge that he relayed most effectively to his son.

*German Bernard Langer had back to back wins at the 1986 Masters and Heritage.*

A satisfactory first-round one-under-par 70 drew little attention to Love. After all, he was six shots behind pacesetter Mark Hayes who came in with a sparkling 64. Love was well down the roster, with many top-notch players firmly entrenched between him and the leader.

Observers began to notice that he was exhibiting surprising finesse for a newcomer, especially with his short game and putting. Still, he did not seem a likely contender for the title when he commenced the final round four off the lead held by Gene Sauers and Steve Jones. After eight holes, Love had lost a stroke to Sauers. When Jones slipped with a double bogey on the eighth hole, it looked like Sauers' tournament. Over the back nine, however, Sauers' game began to deteriorate, while both Love and Jones got red hot. At the 18th tee, Steve Jones needed merely a par four to win his first PGA Tour title.

Such was not to be, however. A misguided three wood off the 18th tee faded out of bounds and left Jones winding up with a double-bogey six. Meanwhile, Love played the 18th aggressively off the tee, feeling that he needed a birdie to win, followed by a six-iron approach which left him a long putt of about 50 feet. All golfers know — even the pros — that a putt of this span at such a crucial moment takes on a mental image of double that length. As Love admitted later, "It looked like a long way. It was one of the best putts I've hit under pressure, but I was glad to have a tap-in." His 271 score brought Love his first Tour victory.

For sheer emotion, no other Heritage equalled the tournament played one year later. The key player in the human drama was Greg Norman who, quite out of character, was brusque and somber when he arrived at Harbour Town in 1988. Unbeknownst to him at the time, another arrival was one Jamie Hutton, a 17-year-old teenager from Menona, Wisconsin, who was afflicted with leukemia and was to undergo a crucial bone marrow transplant the following week. Having made it known that his most fervent desire as a youthful golfer was to meet Greg Norman, he had been flown to Hilton Head by a charitable group that grants the wishes of dying or critically ill children.

Some sensational golf was played that week, but in the final analysis, the real story was one involving Jamie and "The Shark." Nothing since Arnold Palmer's victory in 1969 had so excited the spectators and millions of television watchers as the drama which unfolded when Jamie met "Mr. Norman" Friday morning. But no one could foresee that, in the final round, Jamie would prove to be the real catalyst in the narrative, inspiring Norman to a spectacular final-round 66 and victory.

The Huttons had planned to leave Saturday, after the meeting. But Greg

Norman, deeply affected by the young man's plight and his touching wish, chartered a plane to take Jamie back to Wisconsin after the final round. Not only was this a magnificent gesture on Norman's part, but it proved to have some totally unexpected consequences. Norman was trailing by four strokes as he entered the final round, perhaps too many to make up in a single day's play, especially with David Frost, Gil Morgan, and Chip Beck all surging for the lead.

Warming to both the intensity and human relations aspects of the occasion, Greg had arranged with a photographer friend of his to provide some film equipment and an arm band to Jamie so he could walk inside the ropes. Jamie followed every step of the way while the Shark was inspired to a spectacular final round 66 and victory. Aware of the drama unfolding, the CBS cameramen didn't miss a beat, focusing their lenses on Jamie and Greg as the latter marched on to victory. "It's difficult to put into words," said Norman later. "It's a very emotional win for me and the country. Jamie gave me pointers in a different way. He got me pumped up."

It was the end of the decade, and Payne Stewart was not about to enter a tournament where, in 1983, he had failed to make the cut and a year later had finished dismally in a tie for 48th. But at the last moment, the personable young player who re-introduced knickers to the modern generation, decided he would go to Harbour Town — a course he had declared was "unsuitable" to his style of play — purely as a means of honing his game for the Nabisco Championship, also to be held on the Harbour Town Golf Links later that year.

By 1989, Payne had conquered his wildness off the tee, a tendency which had caused trouble in his earlier play at Harbour Town. He was so steady, in fact, that he established his pace early in the game with a first-round 65, continuing his fine play throughout as a wire-to-wire winner, a feat previously accomplished only by Arnold Palmer, Johnny Miller, Jack Nicklaus and Tom Watson.

The only question from round to round appeared to be whether his injured back would hold out. This situation

*Greg "The Shark" Norman has been a Hilton Head crowd pleaser since the mid 1980s.*

became critical when a rain delay on Saturday left Stewart with seven more holes to be traversed Sunday morning to finish his round. Playing 25 holes in one day is not recommended for back sufferers. Nevertheless, Payne started the final round with a three-stroke lead and was never challenged. A final-round 69 left Stewart with a 16-under-par score of 268, a new tournament record.

*Greg Norman and young Jamie Hutton touched the hearts of America during Norman's inspiring televised triumph in 1988.*

The new decade began with another impressive Heritage milestone, as Payne Stewart returned in 1990 to defend his title. Although he finished eight strokes higher than his course record the previous year, it was enough to place him in a three-way tie - the first in Heritage history - with Larry Mize and Steve Jones. In the playoff, both Stewart and Mize birdied the 17th, but Jones missed the green and was eliminated. The knicker-clad Stewart watched as Mize missed a 20-footer on the 18th. Then, with a very perceptible look of determination, he sank his own 18-foot putt for a win. More significantly, he achieved an unprecedented back-to-back championship.

By 1991, the once unheralded Davis Love, III, was on everyone's tongues as a top favorite. He did not disappoint the fans, despite a few tense moments. He held a three-stroke lead going into the final round and boosted it to four before breaking stride with a triple bogey on the eighth that brought him down the stretch in a dual with Ian Baker-Finch. They battled stroke for stroke until the 17th, when Baker-Finch fell one behind with a bogey, then two behind on the 18th with another bogey. Love held par and thus became the seventh player to achieve two victories at Harbour Town.

By 1992, Love was looking for both a back-to-back victory and a third Heritage title. But he always had a disarming air of modest competence, which made us wonder whether he could really achieve such an impressive distinction. His play here had surely demonstrated very forcefully his mastery of the difficult Harbour Town Links. But could he repeat his victory? No one had ever done this before - it was the burning question on all our minds.

A first round four-under-par 67 gave the defending champion a one-stroke lead over Ed Humenik, Lanny Wadkins, Brad Faxon, and Bruce Fleisher. Another 67 on the second round left him tied with Mark O'Meara and Chip Beck at eight under par. Continuing his spectacularly steady play, he again fired a 67 in the third round to move to 12-under-par 201 and a three stroke lead over O'Meara.

Love's constant application of pressure proved too great for the competition on the fourth day. O'Meara faded and Chip Beck, who started the day four behind, remained in that position to capture second place behind Love's 269, a total which was only one stroke behind Payne Stewart's course record three years earlier. Love thus not only matched Payne's back-to-back victories, but also became the first three-time winner at Harbour Town.

In 1993, entering the MCI Heritage Classic for the twelfth time, David Edwards was not considered a likely winner. Winner of the 1978 NCAA Championship, he was beginning his fifteenth year on TOUR. True, his record had been quite satisfactory, averaging over a quarter of a million dollars in earnings over the past seven years. Yet, he was not considered in the top star category that historically wins at Harbour Town. David Edwards' first TOUR victory was in 1980 playing with his brother Danny in the Walt Disney World National Team Championship. In 1984, he was the winner at the Los Angeles Open firing a magnificent seven under par 64 in the final round to win by three strokes.

*Davis Love III was dominant in the early 1990s.*

Displaying improving skills, Edwards won the prestigious Memorial Tournament in June of '92, finishing in darkness to defeat Rick Fehr on the second extra hole. This victory should have been fair warning for the prognosticators of the 1993 MCI Heritage Classic winner. Perhaps we were all too busy considering a possible four-peat win for Davis Love III.

Always a threat, Payne Stewart was at six under par 65 in the first round holding a one shot lead over four other golfers which did not include Edwards who shot a 68.

David Edwards' 66 in the second round brought him to a tie with David Frost and Bernhard Langer at eight under par 134, just one stroke ahead of Stewart and Bob Estes. The highly competitive nature of the competition was best illustrated that 78 players were able to make the lowest cut score in Heritage history, one-over-par 143.

Edwards, Frost and Paul Azinger were all tied at 9 under-par 204 after the third round, one ahead of John Cook. Asked to handicap the tri-leaders going into the final round play, Edwards commented, "I have won the least (tournaments)".

But, none of his more victiorious challengers were up to the task. Edwards made three birdies and two bogeys on the front nine finishing with one under 35. A similar type of play on the backside resulted in four birdies and three bogeys for a final round two under 69 and a tournament total of 273. Frost shot an even par 71 to finish in second with a 275 total. Azinger's uncharacteristic final round 73 left him at 277 and in a five way tie for third place.

David Edwards' win brought him $202,500 and raised his career earnings to $2,569,176, then ranking #3 on his full-season career money list just behind 1992 ($515,070) and 1991 ($396,695). Number 2 in driving accuracy (79.9%) and tied for fourth in greens and regulations (71.8%) starting play in the MCI Heritage Classic, it is reasonable to predict that the excellent play displayed at the Heritage will portend much continued success for David Edwards in the future.

## UPDATE

The 1994 MCI Heritage Classic will long be remembered as a record-breaking birdie bash played under perfect weather conditions.

Both fans and golfers alike basked under sunny, windless skies as the well-manicured Harbour Town Golf Links was brought to its knees by the world's greatest shotmakers. A cascade of breath-taking drives, chips and putts rattled off their booming artillery as no less than 114 rounds were recorded in the 60s.

Each day the leaderboard flashed more red numbers than the National Treasury, signifying a terrifying assault on the famed Links course's par of 71. And almost hourly, a new leader vaulted to the fore leaving the gallery buzzing as it got caught up in the unfolding drama.

Early-on, it was Bob Estes and Fred Funk firing six-under par 65s on opening day to grab a one-shot lead over the recently-hot Tom Lehman and the genial veteran, Barry Jaeckel.

Though the temperature was in the low 80's, Friday was all Frost at Harbour Town, as David unloaded the greatest round in history in the shadow of the Lighthouse—-a 31-30-61 shaving two strokes off the course record. "A 59 crossed my mind on 15," a happy Frost said later, "but there was too much going on to figure." He had to settle for the breathtaking 61 and an 11-under 131 for a one-stroke lead over Jim McGovern and Larry Mize, both of whom blazed around in 65 blows. Seventy-five players made the cut at 1-over par 143, tieing the tournament record.

*Surprise winners Bob Goalby (above) in 1970, and Doug Tewell (below) in 1980.*

Two former champions, Hale Irwin and Greg Norman, vaulted to the top during the third round, firing a 65 and 67 respectively. With it, Hale, who had previously donned the plaid jacket in 1971 and '73 when he was just a struggling youngster on the PGA TOUR, took command over Greg and southpaw Russ Cochran, with a 54-hole tournament record total of 198.

The perfect weather pattern continued Sunday, as Norman, hot early, caught Irwin after three holes, and then took what looked like an insurmountable three-stroke edge after six.

Hale picked up a shot before the turn, then birdied 12 and 13 to knot matters again. The co-leaders, paired together, matched pars on 14, before Irwin's magnificent iron play took charge. Hale birdied both 15 and 16, almost sinking his tee shot on the latter hole to take a two-shot lead. Now in command, Irwin was content to par his way in to match Norman and capture his third plaid jacket with a new tournament record of 266. Norman parred the last dozen holes to fall short as Hale stormed home in a four-under 31 over the back nine.

"After the first six holes," beamed Irwin afterwards, "I had both feet in the grave. But I kept referring back to the '90 U.S. Open (which Hale rallied to win) to

*In 1973 Hale Irwin's winning prize money was $30,000. Twenty years later David Edwards won $202,500 by finishing first.*

just take one shot at a time. I hit some great iron shots on the second nine."

It was an extremely popular victory as the gallery all hailed Hale Irwin for his magnificent comeback, first catching Norman, then putting him away by two strokes to receive the winner's check of $225,000, another tournament record.

Lee Trevino included the fifteenth at Harbour Town in his list of "Dream Course Holes," in part because of its beautiful overhanging palms and pines, but also because it is "so long even King Kong couldn't get on the green in two."

The British poet, Alfred, Lord Tennyson, wrote in one of his most famous poems, *Morte d'Arthur*, " . . .the old order changeth, yielding place to the new." Nowhere is this theme better illustrated than when comparing the relationships and importance of sponsors in 1969, when the Heritage began, with the period 25 years later at the completion of the Silver Anniversary.

In 1969, at the first Heritage, Delta Airlines, Coca-Cola, and Karp Motors, which was a Chrysler dealership, were all tournament sponsors. The degree of their sponsorship was important, but mainly in terms of providing services "in kind." For example, Delta contributed extensive advertising in the public press, as well as in its own in-flight magazine, which it publishes and distributes to passengers on jetliners. After spectator tickets were totally

*With the arrival of MCI as title sponsor, the tournament found solid footing.*

sold out on Saturday of the first tournament, there was a moment of panic when the administration officials realized there were none available for Sunday. One of the sponsors, Delta Airlines, saved the day when, through its Atlanta printer, the airline was able to get immediate service for the printing of additional tickets, and then had them delivered well before the start of play on Sunday. For its part in the early proceedings, the Coca-Cola Company scheduled an advertising campaign, locally and regionally, as well as supplying beverages for the players and their entourages. And Chrysler, through its Karp Motors dealership in Savannah, Georgia, made available a fleet of automobiles for use by the players at the tournament.

All of these efforts were important and certainly greatly appreciated by the Heritage management. However, the only provider of substantial financial backing — hard dollars, that is — was the Sea Pines Company. By 1975, arrangements had been made with the Drexel Heritage Furniture Company, which had joined Sea Pines and Delta as a tournament sponsor, to provide valuable advertising before and during Heritage week. Drexel also agreed to underwrite a "Closest-to-the-Pin"

*Victories by young sensations like Johnny Miller in 1972 and 1974 captured media attention, attracting national sponsors.*

contest on the 17th hole during the final round of play. Mike Schlueter, a little-known pro from Clover, South Carolina, was a sentimental favorite and a likely one to win this prize, since his tee shot early in the day of that round was just over three feet from the pin. Moreover, he was a young newlywed who would have been an ideal recipient since the prize was a room of furniture, which would have been a welcome gift to present to his bride. As luck would have it, however, the eventual tournament winner, Jack Nicklaus, playing in the final group of the day, hit a shot just a couple of inches inside of Schlueter's marker and captured the prize, valued at some $8,000. The ill-fated Schlueter not only lost the furniture, but finished third from last.

Although the above-mentioned sponsors and others continued to be valuable assets to the Heritage, Sea Pines was still the only supporter providing cash. Money became an ever-increasing problem, what with tournament purses and other costs continuing to rise and financial difficulties developing for the sponsoring Sea Pines Company. Somehow, though, everyone managed to hang on doggedly, and it was not until after 15 years of play that the Heritage Classic became financially viable and profitable.

The year 1987 became a banner one in the financial history of the Heritage Classic. Three important events occurred:

1. In January, the MCI Communications Corporation announced that its board of directors had agreed to sponsor the Heritage Classic for four years, with an option to continue as sponsor for an additional four years. MCI agreed to pay $400,000 to sponsor the event in 1987, increasing the payment in subsequent years to $600,000 by 1991. In addition, MCI's President, Bert C. Roberts, Jr., announced that MCI's financial commitment would not stop there, but that his corporation would be paying for national commercials on CBS television, as well as tying in company incentive and sales programs to the tournament. Some 350 people were brought to the island for the company's annual sales conference the week before the tournament, at which time Roberts announced that the company would transport some of its largest customers to the island for the annual occasion.

2. The Heritage Classic Foundation, a non-profit corporation, was established to own and operate the Heritage Classic. Pro-Am entry fees may be called part of the sponsoring function, crucial for the Heritage or any other tournament. Since the 1987 entry fee for player participants was $1,750 and 180 admissions were sold, the total gross income was a substantial $315,000 for the Pro-Am event alone.

3. Sea Pines Associates, a company wholly owned by Sea Pines property owners, gained ownership of major properties in the plantation, including the Harbour Town Golf Links, through purchase from the bankrupt Hilton Head Holdings Company. This purchase had a significant and beneficial effect on the economics of the Heritage tournament and the effectiveness of its policies of

administration.

These were indeed healthy developments for everyone concerned, taking into consideration the fact that the Heritage is a great boon to local businesses and that it helps to generate more real estate leads and sales in one week than any other comparable period all year long. Exposure is an enormous benefit, both to sponsors and to Hilton Head itself. "In addition to all the businesses that come to the island to watch the tournament, you have the top executives of all the sponsors," said

*Tournament hospitality and marketing exposure have made the tournament one of South Carolina's most prestigious events.*

Charles Bacon, former chairman of the board of Sea Pines Associates. "MCI brings in top people from all over the country, and so do other sponsors like Coca-Cola and Cadillac. These people are exposed to the idea of inviting their customers to the island for business meetings, but also to purchase homes for themselves. I believe that MCI transports more than 400 of its best associates here as a goodwill gesture, but also as part of a genuine advertising promotion for the company. These are top-drawer people — the kind of people you like to know may be considering Hilton Head as a place to retire."

Although golf fans, along with other sports fans, recognize that sponsorship is vital to the economy of the nation's major sporting events, few are aware of the magnitude of such undertakings and the immense capital involved. According to a front-page headline in the sports section of USA Today, June 16, 1993, sponsorship is "the name of the game." The editorial pointed out that sponsors "contribute five times as much as fans to stage U.S. sports events. Sponsors make sports bigger, richer, and more telegenic as they wage the priciest competition in sports: the scramble for fans' brand loyalties." Unfortunately for the fans, though, as the article conceded, "sponsor contributions don't mean lower ticket prices."

> "You rarely hear anything negative said about Harbour Town. That's because it's a fair test of golfing skills."
>
> *Tom Watson, Heritage winner in 1979 and 1982 and five-time leading money winner on the PGA Tour.*

The article went on to report that "Spending on sponsorship has grown much faster than spending in more traditional ad channels, increasing annually by an average of 30% over the last ten years compared with single-digit average annual increases in overall advertising or promotional spending. And often, sponsorship fees are just the beginning. Companies might spend two or three times the amount of the fees on promotions to make the public aware of its tie-in."

The contributions of all sponsors have certainly been most helpful — even dramatically so — in the continuing successful operation of the MCI Classic.

*CBS has covered the tournament since the mid 1970s, and has routinely earned one of the best audience shares on the PGA TOUR.*

Without sponsors, the tournament simply could no longer exist. The very satisfactory relationship between the Heritage and its principal, MCI, is unique.

It may surprise some, but at the time this sponsorship was established, both the Heritage and MCI had significant problems. As has been recounted earlier, the property-owner corporation, Sea Pines Associates, was just taking over from the bankruptcy court the remains of the formerly successful Sea Pines Company, an enterprise that had fallen into bankruptcy in the years following the Fraser family sale of 1983. There was no assurance that the new property-owned company would be successful, yet the financial situation seemed more promising.

It was not a reassuring break in the timing as far as MCI was concerned either, since the corporation faced some rather severe economic problems.

After the court-oriented breakup of the giant AT&T Corporation in 1982, MCI was formed to take on the highly competitive giant in the field of long-distance telephone service. Although MCI continued to be increasingly successful in this field, there was no certainty of a future profitable operation at the time the first contract with the Heritage was signed in 1987. In blunt terms, the courtship of MCI and the Heritage posed many tricky questions.

Complicating the situation was the health crisis facing the dynamic founder and Chief Executive Officer of MCI, Bill McGowan.

Despite health problems, he was especially interested in the tournament until his death in 1992. He strongly believed that MCI's sponsorship of this particular tournament provided significant promotional value and good will. Too much cannot be said about Bill McGowan and the excellent relationship he established between MCI Telecommunications Corporation and the Heritage Classic. His contributions and cooperation were indispensable to the event's continued success.

Fortunately, Bill had trained a very competent and well-coordinated management team. His close associate, Bert C. Roberts, Jr., who took over as chairman, was on hand to fulfill his plans for steady growth and financial health. Both of these corporate officers expressed the belief that the sponsorship of the Heritage, with its prestige, strong field, and philanthropic goals, was beneficial to its own image and growth.

All of those who manage the annual Harbour Town event are convinced they offer top quality to MCI, or any other sponsor interested in maintaining a bright, credible image through association with the golf tournament, the PGA

*The golf tournament has grown beyond Sea Pines to a national extravaganza.*

TOUR and the world-renowned vacation destination of Hilton Head Island. Tennyson's "old order" may have changed, but the new one is better and stronger than ever.

*National sponsors have flocked to the tournament in the 1990s.*

# CHAPTER 6
# THE SUPPORTING CAST

The date is November 28, 1969. The time is early morning, around 7:30. Bill Dyer, executive director of the first Heritage Golf Classic, is standing in the back of the ninth green. Vance Fowler is talking to him about the opening of the tournament the previous day, and they agree that it has been truly remarkable that such a big event could have started so smoothly.

After telling Bill how well he had done, Vance said, "There's only one improvement I could propose, that you station someone at the ninth green to introduce players as they came past the clubhouse gallery.

Bill looked at Vance with a big, bright smile. "A great idea! Can you start today?"

Vance protested that he had no experience in golf tournament announcing, but that he would give it a try. If it worked, he'd continue the next day. Twenty-five years later, Vance could look back on many happy and memorable moments as a volunteer. Except for that first day of the first tournament, he never missed a day.

*Live satellite transmissions provide worldwide coverage directly from Harbour Town.*

Vance became but one in the army known as the Heritage Volunteers which, as Bob Little, former Men's Chairman, described as "...essential to the success of the golf tournament. To state it more plainly: no volunteers, no tournament!"

Fewer than 200 assisted as volunteers with the first Heritage in 1969. By the early 1990s that number was pushing one thousand.

Tournament officials over the years have strongly emphasized the importance of these unpaid assistants from the standpoint of both efficiency and cost. If it had ever been necessary that individuals be hired to perform the duties of volunteers, it would have been next to impossible to find available people with the essential skills. For the most part, these volunteers are golfers themselves, and are well aware of the manner in which their duties should be performed. It has been estimated that, even if paid workers with adequate skills could be obtained, the cost would be prohibitive — well over a quarter of a million dollars for each tournament.

*Traditions have been maintained as part of the tournament's growth.*

From the start, it was obvious that the whole undertaking would have to lean heavily on a legion of workers who would commit themselves to providing labor, skills and money, with no expectation of recompense, other than the personal satisfaction of being involved with the tournament. The tournament's planners counted on a hidden asset: the determination and allegiance of Hilton Head Islanders to make the tournament the best on the PGA TOUR.

Today, the volunteer organization is complex, yet tightly knit. The general chairman, a volunteer himself, is the coordinator of all the volunteer committees. He serves as liaison with the tournament director (who is a salaried executive and Foundation board member), works with them to fill the needs of the tournament and coordinate functions with the PGA TOUR.

J.W. (Buddy) McDill was the first organizer of volunteers and was general chairman from the first tournament in 1969 until he retired in 1987. Paul Freeman became general chairman in 1987 and remained until his death in October 1988 when Brian Hennessey took over and served to 1990, including the Nabisco Championships of 1989.

The current chairman, Brigadier General Howard E. "Doc" Kreidler, (U.S. Air Force, retired) started as a volunteer marshal in 1972. "The volunteers are a dedicated and highly qualified group," he notes. "Each year, we have several newcomers who are quickly indoctrinated by a large number of old-timers, many of whom have been performing for several years." In fact, six persons are on record as having served at all of the tournaments during the first quarter-century of the Heritage: Dickie Englehart, Lawton Englehart, Vance Fowler, Marion McDuffie, Mike Johnson and Emily Parkhurst.

It would take dozens, if not hundreds of pages to list the volunteers who have, over the years, made this event not only a highly organized but enjoyable tournament for players and fans. Volunteers come from all walks of life and, although unpaid, they work tirelessly. You will find retirees, housewives, native islanders, all races, colors and creeds make the tournament a big success.

We would be remiss, however, if we did not take note of those volunteers who have taken on the additional burdens and responsibilities as chairpersons. Unfortunately early tournaments do not provide written records of volunteer committees. The organizers of this manuscript had to rely on individual memories. There may be some chairpersons mistakenly left off the list. If so, we offer our apologies in advance.

## VOLUNTEER COMMITTEES

### MEN'S CHAIRMAN

Under the general chairman, duties are shared by separate men's and ladies' chairpersons. The designations are somewhat misleading, however, since both sexes are represented in each group and in the committees under them. MCI's chairmen have included H.E. Kreidler, Robert Little, Bob Cleary.

## MARSHALS

Approximately 250 marshals are on duty to handle crowd control during the tournament, with a team of six to eight marshals required at each hole. Marshals chairmen have included: Major General Eddie Baston, Jr., Karl Kellerman, Paul Freeman, Al Wolff, Glen Offensend, John Allyn, Tom Baker, Richard Lorbach, Jim Norbury, Max Stein and Jack Richards.

## SCORING - LEADERBOARDS

Until 1980, leaderboards were manual and placed every two or three holes around the course. Today, with electronic scoreboards, some sixty-eight persons (approximately thirty-four ladies, thirty-four men) collect scores from the markers at each hole and call scores in to Scoring Central. Chairpersons have included: Elredge Leeming, Merle Graham, Jim Gates, Ed Warner, Charles Steingrabar, Maury Parker.

*Mike Stevens (shown above with radio) has earned a reputation as one of the best tournament directors on the PGA TOUR.*

## SCORING CENTRAL

Located in a room under the clubhouse, a crew of about eighteen men and women, coordinate the collection and posting of scores phoned in from the course. Data are written on master sheets and then keyed into a computer, which transmits this information to the electronic leaderboards. CBS also picks up this information for use during the network's broadcasts. Chairpersons have included: Howard E. Kreidler, Mrs. H.E. Kreidler, Major Willis, Bob Killingsworth, Jim Dean.

## TRANSPORTATION - SHUTTLE

This group provides for the volunteer workers themselves a continuous transit service between the patron parking lot, the thirteenth green volunteer lot, and the volunteer lot at Greenwood Circle.

The weather committee provides "safe haven" houses and other shelters near the tees and greens for pros, caddies, markers and standard bearers during rain delays, until PGA officials call for either resumption or suspension of play. Whenever a notification of delay is received, the marshal hole captain escorts his playing group to its "safe haven," marked by fluorescent flags. Chairmen have included Paul Leimbeck and Bob Cleary.

## OPENING CEREMONIES

The first Heritage was marked by innovative ceremonial events that have since become traditional. It begins with a parade composed of the Citadel Bagpipe Band, flag bearers, and selected participants, such as golf champions, Heritage Classic Foundation members, sponsors, committee chairmen, and volunteers who march from Harbour Town to the eighteenth green for the ceremonial cannon shoot.

*No professional tournament has a more dramatic introduction.*

Two men dressed in authentic pre-Revolutionary War uniforms load and fire an antique smooth-bore, muzzle-loader cannon, while at the same moment, the current MCI Classic champion drives a golf ball into Calibogue Sound, using a replica of an ancient club hand-crafted by Scotsman Lauri Auchterlonie.

At the beginning of 1969, Fred Wilkins organized these important ceremonial activities, working with an ever-increasing staff of coordinators until he retired twenty-three years later. The cannon shoot alone requires eight volunteers, who make provisions for the band, produce signs and organize the participants. General Walter Higgens and Ed Gibbons have also chaired this group.

## SHOOT-OUT

The Merrill-Lynch Shoot-Out is held at eighteen PGA TOUR events during the year. Conducted on Tuesday of tournament week, the ten-man competition covers nine holes of play in a popular and relaxed event. The field is made up of the top four money winners of the previous year's PGA TOUR money list, the top three money winners from the season-long shoot-out series, and three sponsor selections. Chairmen have included General James Keller, John Elliott and Howard Neleigh.

## LADIES CHAIRPERSON

Slightly over 400 volunteers, mostly women but not all, serve under the overall leadership of the Ladies Chairperson. Macy Ellen Mulford was the first chairperson. Others have included: Vi Vilas, Peggy Trew, Jane Young and Bobbie Kelsey.

## MARKERS

This is by far the largest group in terms of numbers in the ladies' committees, numbering about 130 volunteers. To be a marker requires not only physical agility, but an excellent knowledge of the rules of golf.

One or two markers walk with every group of players, close enough to see individual shots. At the first tee, they write the colors of each golfer's clothing beside his name, to speed player identification. The markers record each shot on the statistic sheet then, at the exit gates of the greens, write each golfer's score for the hole on a marker's pad and give this sheet to the leaderboard reporter who calls the numbers into central scoring. They then update the standard bearer's sign to show each golfer's tournament standing against par.

The PGA TOUR began a statistics program in 1980, providing markers with scoring sheets on which to track each shot. Sent directly to a PGA official at the end of play, a computer program scans in the information which then calculates statistics on each player and each round. Chairpersons have included: Annie Dow, Emma Lee Williams, Helen Means, Marj Fowler and Gordie Rudd.

## TRANSPORTATION

During the first ten years of the Heritage, many pros and some PGA officials had no cars. Transportation to and from their residences, the market, the post office, restaurants, recreational areas, and elsewhere was provided informally by friends and volunteers. Today, of course, most pros have courtesy cars, and the ladies' transportation group, about 165 strong, takes care of other transit needs. Chairpersons of this committee have included: Bo Hedeman, Dorothy Hatch, June Beck and Mrs. E.H. Hall. Shuttle chairpersons have included: Neal Morgan, Robert DellaBovi and Mr. & Mrs. Neil Citron.

## STANDARD BEARERS

Beginning in 1974, standard bearers accompanied each group of players on the final rounds of play. The standards display the current score of each player in the group as it advances from hole to hole.

Because the job is physically demanding, it is generally assigned to husky high school students. Carrying a rather heavy sign five miles on a windy day can be a real challenge. About eighty young people are needed for each tournament. Marge Berrigan, Nancy Schneider and Bill Evans have chaired this group.

*Volunteers perform a wide variety of tasks to make the tournament run effectively.*

## NURSERY

Few spectators are aware of an institution that has become part of the tournament's tradition: the nursery, claimed to be the first on the PGA Tour. Since the Heritage was emphasized as a "family" tournament from the beginning, considerations had to be made for the families who accompanied the pros. Arrangements were relatively simple in the early days, involving lists of experienced babysitters and guides to facilities for toddlers and young children. As the importance of this operation increased, villas were rented by the tournament director and a paid staff took care of the children, while volunteers were recruited as needed. By 1987, the nursery had become essentially an all-volunteer project. Chairpersons have included: Robin Stevens, Marge Dornirer, Helen Cleary, Holly Pedersen and Mrs. Hardy Tuten.

## COURIERS

Couriers are in the thick of the action, from start to finish as they drive golf carts to transport the players, caddies, markers and standard bearers from the eighteenth green to the clubhouse, either at the end of their play or between nines when play begins on both one and ten. Judy Capers and Mrs. J. Luther Heard have served as chairpersons.

## MAINBOARD SCORING AND PRESS TENT

Scorers receive scorecard printouts from the ninth hole and player scorecards from the 18th hole. Scores are checked as well as players' signatures. Then they are read to the PGA calligrapher who writes them on the big board.

Special drama always occurs at the mainboard on Friday as the countdown for the cut unfolds. The low 70 and ties remain in the tournament, with others having only the next tournament week to look forward to. Often the cut score depends on the last few scorecards. Sometimes, if the cut score goes up or down by only a single stroke, as many as fifteen players could be tied.

A similar process takes place in the large press room. Writers may actually see only a small portion of the tournament action spread over eighteen holes. More information is available within the press tent than on the course, so the accuracy and timeliness of the press tent scoring and leaderboard is of major importance. Marian Dawson served as chairperson for 16 years. Annalou Thomas has been chairperson for mainboard scoring since 1984 and Mary Murdock chairperson for the press tent. Scoring chairpersons for the 9th and 18th holes have been: Edward C. Ward, Peter Bauman, Wilbur Collier, Joe Lewis, John Semmes, Alex Thomsen, Ned B. Williams, John Mingay, J. William Cole.

*Live radio broadcasts keep everyone informed on a continuing basis.*

## REGISTRATION

While the primary task is registering pro-golfers and pro-am contestants and dispensing information, the registration staff handles a variety of requests.

A player shortly due on the tee discovered some repair work was urgently needed on his trousers. A volunteer sent her husband home for her sewing kit, quickly stitched the seam and the player arrived at the tee just in time. Now needles and thread are included in the supply list. Registration chairpersons have included Harriett McDill, Vi Vilas, Rosalyn Wilson, Mary Ruth Holmes, Betsey Kennedy,

In 1984, the American Society of Golf Course Architects selected the top three "best-designed" golf courses in the USA. Their selection of those constructed before 1962:

*Cypress Point Club,*
*Pebble Beach, CA*
*Peachtree Golf Club,*
*Atlanta, GA*
*Pine Valley Golf Club,*
*Clementin, NJ*

Best three courses built after 1962:

*Harbour Town Golf Links*
*Hilton Head Island, SC*
*Sentryworld Golf Club*
*Stevens Point, WI*
*The Vantage Club (Desert)*
*Indian Wells, CA*

Marie Hayman, Lori Leaman, Meg Smith and Mrs. James Lowie.

## UNIFORM COMMITTEE

The committee arranges for a supply of uniform items and cheerfully dispenses these to the 900 plus volunteers over the several weeks before the tournament. The two days immediately preceding the start are not only hectic but at times amusing, as is illustrated by a lady volunteer who, when told the hats were "one size fits all" tried on twenty-one of them before making a selection and driving off to her duties. Chairpersons have included Margie Crawford and Marian McDuffie.

## OTHER KEY VOLUNTEER COORDINATORS HAVE INCLUDED:

*Parking:* Col. Robert Kriwanek, John Kellum, A.R. Hooker, Jr., Arthur Hedeman.

*Concessions:* David Bachelder, Steve Gladden and Angie Taylor.

*Caddies:* Don Phillip, H.L. Giles, John Rooley, John Graham, Tom Krebs, Don McGaughey.

*Pro Am:* Gen. Tom Corwin, Russell W. Billman, Brian Hennessey, Art Benzle.

*Media:* Tom Wilson, Arnie Burdick.

*Volunteer Announcers:* Vance Fowler, Elliott Steadman, Leo Beckman and Charles Perry.

> ■ "Hell, it might be an 86 tomorrow, but at least I shot 66 today on one of the greatest courses in the world."
>
> *Lee Trevino in 1983, after completing his first Heritage round with a course-record-matching 30 on the back nine.*

*By the early 1990s the tournament was a sell out.*

## IN CLOSING

Approximately one hundred volunteers perform duties outside the scope of the committee structure, working directly for the tournament director and his staff. Over the years there are many others who have served as advisors, or quietly stepped in to help when they saw the need. These unsung heroes, along with those who have worn the tournament jackets, are deserving of the thanks of all who love golf, the spirit of competition, and Hilton Head Island.

# CHAPTER 7
# A SUMMING UP

Almost from the start, the Heritage was accepted by the pros, and it is generally believed that each year the Heritage attracts one of the strongest fields on the Tour. By way of proof — if such is needed — a listing of the top 100 players in career money earnings, published in the 1993 PGA Tour Media Guide, indicates that every player on this list has participated frequently in the Heritage Classic. Hale Irwin leads the list, having participated in no less than 25! What are the reasons for this unique display of interest in one particular course and one special event?

The first reason is the course itself. The players enjoy the whole playing environment. Harbour Town has been called "A Shotmakers Course," because it is seldom that a round is played without requiring every club in the bag. The narrow fairways and small greens provide a challenge rarely found on the Tour. Furthermore, the course satisfactorily rewards the expertly executed strokes, but, sooner or later, penalizes the wayward efforts. This has been vividly demonstrated during innumerable rounds of championship play.

*Joe Fraser, Jr., Angus Cotton and MCI's Bert C. Roberts, Jr. congratulate Payne Stewart following his exciting sudden death victory in 1990.*

You can just about number on one hand the few players who dislike Harbour Town. Invariably, they are long hitters who are inclined to be a bit wild, the kind of playing style that the course simply does not seem to tolerate. All in all, the course is a major factor in player determination to participate in the Heritage, and it is at its best in mid-April, which is also a favorite time of year for a visit to Hilton Head Island.

Family orientation is another strong drawing card. The Heritage started with an attractiveness for the families of the players in the field and has continued ever since to hold this kind of charm. Hilton Head has not only the ambience that appeals to all ages, but offered something very special when, in 1969, it was able to lure so many away from their much more traditional Thanksgiving holiday. Until that time, few of the pros on the PGA Tour were in the habit of enjoying the novelty of bringing their wives and children to a golf tournament. The fact of the matter was that it cost too much to get into the habit, and, in many cases, the tournament locations were not favorable as vacation localities for all ages. But at Hilton Head Island the pros realized they could spend the money as part of a scheduled holiday, rather than taking a family trip somewhere else. And the magic has endured for more than a quarter of a century.

The people running the Heritage also made certain that the players would be welcome guests on the island, and saw to it that they received the most attractive housing and other amenities at the lowest possible cost and in the finest locations. Walk out your door in one direction, and you were right on the golf course. Head in other directions, and you would be on the tennis courts, at the beach, boating offshore, fishing, or meandering through a wildlife nature preserve.

Hitting the golf ball sometimes gets boring, even for the most avid aficionados of the sport. And, after all, golfing is a business with the pros, and when they finish the day's work, they — like any other professionals — want to relax and enjoy some other form of sport or enjoyment. From the very beginning of the Heritage, Hilton Head acquired a reputation for offering the widest variety of these, and other, recreational activities. Later, as the island developed, new attractions were added to these welcome offerings, including fine restaurants, the performing arts, exhibitions, historic and cultural tours, cycling, oyster roasts, and multitudes of other activities that all spelled "fun." In the early days, when the purse was very limited, many pros were housed by local residents, with the results that many lasting friendships were formed between the islanders and the visitors — relationships that exist to this very day.

*Nearly all of the island makes special preparations for each year's tournament festivities.*

One of the developments that has certainly been very beneficial to the Heritage has been the switch in the tournament's relationship to The Master's at Augusta National. In the first place, scheduling the latter first has moved the Heritage from mid-March, when the weather conditions are generally uncertain, to April, when warm, gentle breezes and sunny skies are more likely. Equally important, as great as The Master's is for players and spectators alike, it is still an emotionally-filled, highly-charged, pressure-packed tournament. Although strong competition and aggressive play are part of the Harbour Town tradition, the Heritage is still a low-key tournament by comparison, offering more opportunities for the players to relax. As has been repeated many times over by top-ranking participants, "The players like this, and most feel that this kind of atmosphere relieves tensions, helps them to play better, and keeps them in finer tune for the next stop on the Tour."

It goes without saying that CBS likes Harbour Town, to a large extent because the tournament directors of the Heritage have a reputation for establishing a close, well-coordinated working relationship with the network — said to be one of the best on the PGA Tour. TV producers have been high in their praise of the locale, the facilities, and the island people they have worked with over the years. Equally important, they could not be happier about the way their jobs are simplified — televising The Master's at Augusta National one week and then moving people and equipment the short distance to the Low Country to set up for the Harbour Town coverage. Transportation problems are almost nil, especially by comparison with most of the other Tour broadcasts, when they have to move equipment and personnel (from 75 to 100 people on the average) thousands of miles and meet almost impossible transmission deadlines. Heritage players like to appear on top-rated television shows and the one provided by CBS is among the best.

A listing of the advantages that lure so many top pros and spectators to the island would not be complete without citing the very real and fundamental prestige that the Heritage enjoys, and has enjoyed right from the beginning. Even TV viewers who are only occasional golf watchers have come to recognize the Heritage's noted trademark, the Harbour Town lighthouse, and are intrigued by the traditional ceremonies, such as the shooting of the cannon, the playing of the bagpipes, and the sight of the past winner driving the ball with an antique club out into Calibogue Sound.

Evaluating the economic picture, the present situation is healthy and the future looks bright. Under the able administration of the Heritage Foundation directors, and Mike Stevens as the tournament director, many of the past fiscal problems have been solved and the financial programs strengthened. "I was the first director at the Heritage who was trained to be an independent manager," Mike explains. "My staff and I recognized that professional sports were undergoing some critical changes, and that these changes applied to golf as well as to other fields. The advent of commercial sponsorship, for example, had become an absolute necessity in order to finance major events. Up to a few years ago, the Heritage had not been oriented to coping with this kind of commercialism, let alone exploiting it in an aggressive manner. So we took the bull by the horns and launched a positive approach to the situation. As a result, we have increased revenues every year during the past decade, working from a budget of about $600,000 to today's when we are eclipsing $3 million." Another indication of the value of the Heritage,as previously alluded to, is the fact that it has a very favorable impact on the economy of South Carolina, a figure that adds up to $22 million in the space of one week, more than any other single event in the entire state.

*Local scholarships are provided by MCI Telecommunications Corp. and the Heritage Foundation.*

In conclusion, we have to consider that the Heritage draws a strong field of contenders because it does offer substantial monetary rewards, even though it is just in the top half of PGA Tour purses. The amounts have gone up steadily, year after year, from the first purse totalling $100,000 to an eleven-fold increase over 25 years to $1,300,000. Everyone concerned with the administration of the tournament fully realizes that it is vital for the Heritage to remain competitive, as well as to offer that certain, sometimes elusive, appeal that attracts contenders and fans alike, year after year.

"To every thing there is a season, and a time to every purpose under the heaven," is the Proverb. Thus it was and is for the MCI Classic golf tournament, a coming together of many elements — the visionary developer of Sea Pines Plantation on a relatively unknown southeastern barrier island employs a dynamic and creative team of golf course designers then reaches for the stars — in this case the stars of the PGA Tour — and touches them.

The Harbour Town Golf Links is a truly great course, and MCI has proven to be a truly great and far-sighted sponsor. But most important of all, Vance Fowler would surely say, is the continuing enthusiastic commitment and support of the Hilton Head Island community who, through their unselfish devotion to the event and the sport, have taken this one event on the PGA Tour and made it into the "classic" it is today ... and will continue to be in years to come.

# APPENDIX
# TOURNAMENT WINNERS

WINNERS, SCORES AND PURSES 1969-1994

## 1969

| | | |
|---|---|---|
| Winner: | Arnold Palmer | 68-71-70-74 - 283 |
| Runners-up: | Bert Yancey | 76-68-70-72 - 286 |
| | Richard Crawford | 71-69-72-74 - 286 |

| | |
|---|---|
| Winner's Prize: | $20,000 |
| Total Purse: | $100,000 |

## 1970

| | | |
|---|---|---|
| Winner: | Bob Goalby | 74-70-70-66 - 280 |
| Runner-up: | Lanny Wadkins | 73-74-69-68 - 284 |
| | (Amateur) | |

| | |
|---|---|
| Winner's Prize: | $20,000 |
| Total Purse: | $100,000 |

## 1971

| | | |
|---|---|---|
| Winner: | Hale Irwin | 68-73-68-70 - 279 |
| Runner-up: | Bob Lunn | 71-68-71-70 - 280 |

| | |
|---|---|
| Winner's Prize: | $22,000 |
| Total Purse: | $110,000 |

## 1972

| | | |
|---|---|---|
| Winner: | Johnny Miller | 71-65-75-70 - 281 |
| Runner-up: | Tom Weiskopf | 71-73-72-66 - 282 |

| | |
|---|---|
| Winner's Prize: | $25,000 |
| Total Purse: | $125,000 |

## 1973

| Winner: | Hale Irwin | 69-66-65-72 - 272 |
| Runners-up: | Jerry Heard | 69-71-67-70 - 277 |
| | Grier Jones | 70-68-71-68 - 277 |

Winner's Prize:     $30,000
Total Purse:        $150,000

## 1974

| Winner: | Johnny Miller | 66-67-72-70 - 275 |
| Runner-up: | Gibby Gilbert | 71-71-68-69 - 279 |

Winner's Prize:     $40,000
Total Purse:        $200,000

## 1975

| Winner: | Jack Nicklaus | 66-63-74-68 - 271 |
| Runner-up: | Tom Weiskopf | 70-65-68-71 - 274 |

Winner's Prize:     $40,000
Total Purse:        $200,000

## 1976

| Winner: | Hubert Green | 68-67-66-73 - 274 |
| Runner-up: | Jerry McGee | 71-69-71-68 - 279 |

Winner's Prize:     $43,000
Total Purse:        $215,000

## 1977

| Winner: | Graham Marsh | 65-72-67-69 - 273 |
| Runner-up: | Tom Watson | 67-67-66-74 - 274 |

Winner's Prize:     $45,000
Total Purse:        $225,000

## 1978

| | | |
|---|---|---|
| Winner: | Hubert Green | 70-70-70-67 - 277 |
| Runner-up: | Hale Irwin | 68-68-73-70 - 279 |

Winner's Prize: $45,000
Total Purse: $225,000

## 1979

| | | |
|---|---|---|
| Winner: | Tom Watson | 65-65-69-71 - 270 |
| Runner-up: | Ed Sneed | 69-69-71-66 - 275 |

Winner's Prize: $54,000
Total Purse: $300,000

## 1980

| | | |
|---|---|---|
| Winner: | Doug Tewell | 69-66-72-73 - 280 * |
| Runner-up: | Jerry Pate | 66-69-73-72 - 280 |

Winner's Prize: $54,000
Total Purse: $300,000

*Tewell won on first hole of playoff*

## 1981

| | | |
|---|---|---|
| Winner: | Bill Rogers | 71-69-68-70 - 278 |
| Runners-up: | Bruce Devlin | 70-71-71-67 - 279 |
| | Craig Stadler | 71-70-71-67 - 279 |
| | Hale Irwin | 68-70-73-68 - 279 |
| | Gil Morgan | 67-72-72-68 - 279 |

Winner's Prize: $54,000
Total Purse: $300,000

## 1982

| | | |
|---|---|---|
| Winner: | Tom Watson | 69-68-72-71 - 280 * |
| Runner-up: | Frank Connor | 71-66-70-73 - 280 |

Winner's Prize: $54,000
Total Purse: $300,000

*Watson won on first hole of playoff*

## 1983

| | | |
|---|---|---|
| Winner: | Fuzzy Zoeller | 67-72-65-71 - 275 |
| Runner-up: | Jim Nelford | 68-68-70-71 - 277 |

| | |
|---|---|
| Winner's Prize: | $63,000 |
| Total Purse: | $350,000 |

## 1984

| | | |
|---|---|---|
| Winner: | Nick Faldo | 66-67-68-69 - 270 |
| Runner-up: | Tom Kite | 68-67-70-66 - 271 |

| | |
|---|---|
| Winner's Prize: | $72,000 |
| Total Purse: | $400,000 |

## 1985

| | | |
|---|---|---|
| Winner: | Bernhard Langer | 68-66-69-70 - 273 * |
| Runner-up: | Bobby Wadkins | 65-68-72-68 - 273 |

| | |
|---|---|
| Winner's Prize: | $72,000 |
| Total Purse: | $400,000 |

*Langer won on first hole of playoff*

## 1986

| | | |
|---|---|---|
| Winner: | Fuzzy Zoeller | 68-68-69-71 - 276 |
| Runners-up: | Roger Maltbie | 67-72-69-69 - 277 |
| | Greg Norman | 70-68-69-70 - 277 |
| | Chip Beck | 70-67-70-70 - 277 |

| | |
|---|---|
| Winner's Prize: | $81,000 |
| Total Purse: | $450,000 |

## 1987

| | | |
|---|---|---|
| Winner: | Davis Love III | 70-67-67-67 - 271 |
| Runner-up: | Steve Jones | 67-66-67-72 - 272 |

| | |
|---|---|
| Winner's Prize: | $117,000 |
| Total Purse: | $650,000 |

## 1988

| | | |
|---|---|---|
| Winner: | Greg Norman | 65-69-71-66 - 271 |
| Runners-up: | Gil Morgan | 71-64-69-68 - 272 |
| | David Frost | 69-64-69-70 - 272 |

| | |
|---|---|
| Winner's Prize: | $126,000 |
| Total Purse: | $700,000 |

## 1989

| | | |
|---|---|---|
| Winner: | Payne Stewart | 65-67-67-69 - 268 |
| Runner-up: | Kenny Perry | 65-67-70-71 - 273 |

| | |
|---|---|
| Winner's Prize: | $144,000 |
| Total Purse: | $800,000 |

## 1990

| | | |
|---|---|---|
| Winner: | Payne Stewart | 70-69-66-71 - 276 * |
| Runners-up: | Larry Mize | 71-69-70-66 - 276 |
| | Steve Jones | 68-73-66-69 - 276 |

| | |
|---|---|
| Winner's Prize: | $180,000 |
| Total Purse: | $1,000,000 |

*Stewart won playoff with birdie on 18th*

## 1991

| | | |
|---|---|---|
| Winner: | Davis Love III | 65-68-68-70 - 271 |
| Runner-up: | Ian Baker-Finch | 75-64-65-69 - 273 |

| | |
|---|---|
| Winner's Prize: | $180,000 |
| Total Purse: | $1,000,000 |

## 1992

| | | |
|---|---|---|
| Winner: | Davis Love, III | 67-67-67-68 - 269 |
| Runners-up: | Chip Beck | 69-65-71-68 - 273 |

| | |
|---|---|
| Winner's Prize: | $180,000 |
| Total Purse: | $1,000,000 |

# 1993

| | | |
|---|---|---|
| Winner: | David Edwards | 68-66-70-69 - 273 |
| Runner-up: | David Frost | 67-67-70-71 - 275 |

Winner's Prize: $202,500
Total Purse: $1,125,000

# 1994

| | | |
|---|---|---|
| Winner: | Hale Irwin | 68-65-65-68 - 266 |
| Runners-up: | Greg Norman | 67-66-67-68 - 268 |

Winner's Prize: $225,000
Total Purse: $1,250,000

*CBS commentators Ken Venturi, (left), and Pat Summerall compare notes after Bill Rogers' 1981 win.*

# PHOTO CREDITS

# BIBLIOGRAPHY

The following books may be of interest to readers who would like more information about the tournament, the Harbour Town Links, and golf on Hilton Head Island:

Bunton, Terry, *The History of the Heritage*, 1969-1989, privately printed. Bluffton, South Carolina, 1989.

Lockwood, Eileen, editor. *Legends Guide to the Golf Courses of Hilton Head Island*. Legends Publications, Hilton Head Island, South Carolina, 1991.

Price, Charles, and Rogers, George C., Jr. *The Carolina Low Country: Birthplace of American Golf 1786*. Sea Pines Company, Hilton Head Island, South Carolina, 1980.

# HERITAGE CLASSIC FOUNDATION
# BOARD OF TRUSTEES

*Some of the Foundation Board of Trustees shown in a 1994 photo -*

*Front Row - left to right: Gov. John West, Paula Bethea, Tom Daniels, Angus Cotton, Francis Webster, Joe Fraser, Dwight Holder, Charles Fraser, Deke DeLoach, Ralph Kuhn, William Verity, Michael Malanick, Peter Bauman.*
*Back Row - left to right: Tom Reilley, Ben Racusin, Cliff Charnes, John Curry, Charles Bacon, Charles Flynn, Jim Coleman, Simon Fraser, John Davis.*

## HERITAGE CLASSIC FOUNDATION BOARD OF TRUSTEES

JOSEPH B. FRASER
CHAIRMAN

CARTHA D. DeLOACH
VICE CHAIRMAN

JOHN F. CURRY
SECRETARY

ANGUS COTTON
TREASURER

MICHAEL D. STEVENS
TOURNAMENT DIRECTOR

J. SIMON FRASER
LEGAL COUNSEL

## TRUSTEES

PAULA H. BETHEA
JAMES P. COLEMAN
ANGUS COTTON
JOHN F. CURRY
THOMAS G. DANIELS
JOHN W. DAVIS
CARTHA D. DeLOACH
JOSEPH B. FRASER
J. SIMON FRASER
RALPH G. KUHN
MICHAEL J. MALANICK
THOMAS D. REILLEY
MICHAEL D. STEVENS
C. WILLIAM VERITY
FRANCIS S. WEBSTER
JOHN C. WEST
JAMES WILKES

## HONORARY TRUSTEES

CHARLES F. BACON
PETER W. BAUMAN
CHARLES W. FLYNN
CHARLES E. FRASER
DWIGHT A. HOLDER
BENJAMIN M. RACUSIN
JOHN H. ZIMMERMAN